MW00979752

ADVANCE PRAISE

"Self-assurance is a requisite to success. Not everyone was born with it, and it isn't easily taught. I highly recommend this book to anyone who struggles with challenges but isn't ready to give up."

—KEVIN LOWE, SIX-TIME NHL STANLEY CUP CHAMPION, HOCKEY HALL OF FAMER, AND FORMER CAPTAIN, COACH, AND GENERAL MANAGER OF THE EDMONTON OILERS

"This book captivated me right from the start! I've always believed that confidence leads to success and that the subject isn't talked about enough. This is not a how-to instruction book. Many books focus on strategies and tactics, but few talk about emotion. Confidence is an emotion. It is a feeling. It's a belief in one's abilities, and you will never succeed if you don't believe in yourself.

"Jeremy humbly takes us through his own journey of working through his struggles, failures, and lack of confidence,

all to create a dream life and sustainable success. His relatable philosophies will challenge you to look deep within yourself and, if you dare to accept, you'll never be the same person again. Read intently from start to finish, or you'll miss the subtle points of wisdom that might just change your life."

—RICHARD ROBBINS, INTERNATIONAL
SPEAKER, AUTHOR, AND CEO OF RRI

"This is an incredible book full of insightful nuggets. It's real. It's raw. It's timely and relevant. It gets inside your heart in a practical way. Jeremy doesn't derive his wisdom from theory. His down-to-earth philosophy and approach to life comes from the school of experience. Within these pages, Jeremy shows us what excellence and true success is about. If you are committed to living your best life—one of courage, confidence, character, and contribution—this book will be a tremendous support to you."

—DAVID IRVINE, LEADERSHIP COACH, BESTSELLING
AUTHOR, AND CEO OF IRVINESTONE

"Witnessing how Jeremy lives his life in the pursuit of excellence and self-mastery is inspiring. With humility and honesty weaving through like a golden thread, Jeremy's book feels like a best friend sitting with you in the hardest of moments, challenging you to see your own truth and greatness and guiding you to live it."

—JULIANNA BOOTSMAN, CEO OF WHITE BOX LEADERSHIP

SELF-ASSURANCE

SELF-ASSURANCE

STRUGGLE, CONFIDENCE, AND SUCCESS

JEREMY AMYOTTE

LIONCREST
PUBLISHING

COPYRIGHT © 2021 JEREMY AMYOTTE
All rights reserved.

SELF-ASSURANCE
Struggle, Confidence, and Success

ISBN   978-1-5445-2011-7 *Hardcover*
       978-1-5445-2010-0 *Paperback*
       978-1-5445-2009-4 *Ebook*

To my sons, Owen and Jaxson. I wrote this for you, just in case...

CONTENTS

INTRODUCTION 11

1. WHO ARE YOU? 23
2. VALUES 31
3. EGO 45
4. DISCIPLINE AND INTEGRITY 63
5. THE GREAT CANADIAN DEATH RACE—DEVELOPING DISCIPLINE... 73
6. COURAGE AND PAIN 87
7. COURAGE LEADS TO CONFIDENCE........................ 99
8. JUMP—A COURAGE CASE STUDY 107
9. COURAGE AND RELATIONSHIPS.......................... 119
10. ACCEPTING RESPONSIBILITY 135
11. HUMILITY 149
12. RESPONSE-ABILITY.. 163
13. INFLUENCE 175
14. SHY AND AWKWARD 185
15. HEALTHY SELF-FOCUS...................................... 199
16. SELF-SABOTAGE 211
17. CHANGING PERSPECTIVES 221
18. EXCELLENCE 231
CONCLUSION 241
ACKNOWLEDGMENTS 245
ABOUT THE AUTHOR 249

INTRODUCTION

———

All I ever wanted was not to struggle. But struggling seemed to be in my DNA, as if it was my predetermined destiny. I thought little of myself as a young boy, and it only got worse as I grew older. Whether I was learning something new, interacting with people, or just generally trying to get through life, nothing came easy to me. I felt alone because everyone around me appeared to have what it took to accomplish what they wanted, while I was stuck wondering why I wasn't better, why *life* wasn't better. Struggle was all I knew, and I hadn't the slightest clue how to break through it.

I grew up in Edmonton, Alberta, Canada, as the youngest of three siblings, whom I'm close to. My parents started their family at the ripe young age of nineteen. Though they were young, they were loving and respectful, and neither ever said or did anything to intentionally hurt us. My mom was a wonderful homemaker, and she made all three of us her main priority. She did her best to keep us active and socialized, and she encouraged us to follow our passions. Dad was the good-looking guy who could pick up any sport and play like a pro. He was also a great salesperson, filled with charisma and talent. I adored being in his company and felt like the luckiest kid in the world when our family was together.

For the first decade of my life, we lived like any other middle-class family. We enjoyed ski trips to the mountains, camping trips, family dinners, Friday movie nights, and all the other awesome stuff that makes up great childhood memories. But, as I would later find out, Dad had a secret. He struggled with an addiction to crack cocaine.

He managed to hide it well over the first few years. He functioned well enough to maintain his day-to-day responsibilities and reserved his habits for the more social hours of the night, thus hardly disrupting his work and escaping the attention of his family. But over the years, he distanced himself from the house, and the family time that we all cherished so much began to fade. When he was home, he wasn't the same person I'd remembered. He was filled with anger, frustration, and intense stress. The happiness and laughter I recalled filling our home in the years past were replaced with distress and shouting—mostly from Dad toward Mom as he paced aimlessly through the hallways, lamenting about everything that was going wrong. I listened to all of it, and I felt his pain, as I could often hear subtle whimpers of grief cracking through the armor of his angry dialogue. The drug had taken over his life, and consequently, it took over ours too.

When I was thirteen, Dad was forced to move out. Mom was left to take care of us alone, and although she was doing her best, her authoritative "because I said so" parenting style didn't mesh well with my rebellious nature. Within a year, I moved out too.

I first moved in with my dad, as he had a condo on the other side of the city. The fridge and pantry were completely empty, and the furniture was minimal. He just had a bed and nightstand in his room, then an old, lumpy couch, a coffee table, and an old television in the living room—the kind that was shaped like a box, with bunny ears that you had to adjust in order to keep the picture from scrambling. None of that mattered much, as Dad forgot to set up an account for electricity, and we eventually lost power. It was as if he had started moving in, but then quit halfway and abandoned the place. Hanging out in a dark, half-empty condo with nothing around me got old fast.

Cell phones weren't a thing yet, and we didn't have a landline, so it left me quite isolated. I also didn't have any money, and neither did Dad. Besides, I had only seen him once in the time I had stayed there, so even if he could manage to spare a few dollars from his habits, I wouldn't have had the chance to ask him for it. Somehow, I found ways to scrape enough money for a bus pass and to keep the kitchen stocked with bread, peanut butter, and jam, which provided me with my daily three meals: breakfast, lunch, and dinner. When I ran out of those food items, I took an earlier bus to school. I would stop at my mom's house on the way to sneak some food from her pantry while she was at work. I didn't think she would mind. Even though I wasn't living with her, I was sure she would still want me to eat.

I could handle the isolation and the lack of resources, as I thought it was a fair trade for my freedom. Every evening, I would walk across the street to the pay phone inside a mall to call my friends and girlfriend. That was until a kid got shot in the mall. That mall always felt like an unsafe spot where I shouldn't hang out. It had a grocery store and a few dingy retail shops. Otherwise, it was just a spot in a bad part of town for all the bad kids to hang out at after school. I didn't feel quite as comfortable there after the shooting, but I didn't want to spend more time than I had to at the condo. Instead, I started hanging around with friends, inviting myself to their parents' homes, and loitering until they'd ask me to leave.

My dad eventually told me that I had to move back in with Mom, as he knew his condo wasn't a good place for me to live. I obliged and moved back home. But that lasted only a few weeks, as I just couldn't get along with my mother. So I packed my schoolbag full of clothes and moved again. I stayed with friends in their parents' homes until I was no longer welcome. Then I would move to another friend's house until their parents asked me to leave too. If I had nowhere to go, I would move back in with my mother, but it never lasted long, as I would quickly be reminded that we just couldn't live together.

Over the years, I continued to struggle. I barely finished high school and went straight to working jobs I wasn't good at with people I didn't get along with. I started a business that never made money but left me with six figures of unsecured debt before I turned twenty-one. I had nothing to show for it and no income to pay it back. I was ashamed of my body. I wasn't good with girls. I had a short fuse and dealt with anger and frustration on a daily basis. I wasn't articulate, and I cowered if any attention was on me. For as much as I wanted to be seen for who I dreamed I could be, I didn't want to be seen for who I really was.

I constantly changed everything in my world while still trying to figure things out. I moved to at least thirty homes in a ten-year span, putting my footprint on every area of the city. I changed jobs, found new friends, and experimented with new substances, but the struggle always followed me. I couldn't fucking get away from it, though I sure kept trying. Eventually, I stumbled upon some advice that set me on a different path. My outside world didn't change that instant, but my thinking did. Then, little by little, life started to improve until, eventually, I was living in a completely different world and I'd become a completely different person. I became quite literally addicted to my own psychology—to how my thinking affects my life. I never ignored what I thought and felt, but I learned to turn negative emotions into positive and productive outcomes. The advice I heard came from a CD recorded by my business coach, Richard Robbins. This introduction to a new way to look at life was the seed of a truth I couldn't ignore. I listened to it over and over until it registered so deeply that it rooted itself as my default way of thinking, pushing out the old ways—the ones that contributed to the struggles and pains I was trying to get away from. This new paradigm, combined with my own experiences and life lessons that followed, became the basis for this book.

A COMMON EXPERIENCE

It turns out that my insecurities are common. Many people have been through much more, and many have been through less. Each one of us is on our own inimitable journey, and despite that, it took me a long time to realize that the inner challenges I faced weren't exclusive to me. Nobody's are. Our experiences in life aren't all the same. We each experience our life challenges at different intensities for different reasons, but every emotion and thought that you and I have felt has also been felt by another. This is what connects us as humans. The trial we face is to find ways to work through our thoughts so we can turn our struggles into genuine successes. Our ability to do so is really the only thing that separates us, and the good news is that everyone is capable of it *if* they allow themselves to trust the process.

I'm not an expert in the field of self-assurance. I don't study it for a living, and I have no official credentials that qualify me to speak about it. In fact, I have no formal degree in anything. I was barely seventeen the last time I stepped foot in a school classroom. But I am an active student, learning as I move through life, studying others, and reflecting often. In doing this, I eventually found a way to become someone that my younger self would never have imagined possible. I found a way to escape the mediocre life I thought I was doomed to live. The road wasn't paved with sunshine and roses, but I learned to turn my deepest fears and insecurities into the very sources of my success. It's not what I have that I'm particularly proud of, but who I've become, the people I've attracted into my life, how I feel, and how I learned to deal with the way I feel. I have come to realize that I'm capable of achieving anything I truly want, and it's a stark contrast to the person I used to be and the life I used to live.

A RESPONSIBILITY TO SHARE

We owe everything we know to those who have shared their findings, their experiences, and their theories. When we learn something important about life that might help another, the responsibility to share isn't limited to formal teachers and other academics. It is everyone's responsibility—yours and mine included. Sharing is responsible for our human progression, and the more of us who do it, the better we evolve. We don't have to start at zero every time, because life is a relay, and those who came before us pass the baton before they go. The insecure person in me asks daily, *Who am I to write on topics of confidence and success? I still struggle with them every day.* But when I get over myself, the voice deeper inside reminds me that, for this very reason, it is my duty to share my experiences, my theories, and my insights because I keep finding ways to conquer my struggles. I learned how to talk and walk myself through insecurities. How you receive this message is up to you, not me. There are no studies to back my theories, as they come from my own personal experiences. If they feel true to you, you'll just know. If they don't, that's okay too.

This book isn't about me or my life story. It's an introspective look at life in general and the common circumstances we all face. I use examples of my own experiences in the hope that you'll relate, but my goal is for you to see life, the people within it, and yourself in a different light. If you struggle with frustrations and find yourself wishing things were easier, I wrote this book for you. If you don't like the way the world works or you simply wish *you* were different, I wrote this book for you. If you're struggling to figure out where you fit in to this world, I wrote this book for you.

I wrote this book for the *me* of twenty years ago because, back then, I believed I was doomed to a mediocre life. I didn't have the skills, charisma, or intelligence to achieve much, and I thought that success was reserved for people who grew up around it, for people lucky enough to be born into it, as if the stars needed to align in a special way—in any way except how they were. It was never enough for someone to tell me that my rationale was bullshit. I had to think my way through it and comprehend it myself. There is a process to it all, and nothing can replace experience for developing a true understanding of anything in life. But to experience something, you have to act, and to act, you need a reason to do so. When you don't believe in a better future, why bother taking the steps that might get you there? Success, as it turns out, requires a journey within. So many of us are afraid of our deepest thoughts because they expose our insecurities. We bury them instead, thinking that is the solution. But, as I found out, uncovering them is the very path to true success.

CONFIDENCE, EXPERIENCE, AND COURAGE

I wasn't aware until later in my journey that confidence is required to get you to a good place. The root of the word is "fid," which is Latin for trust. Therefore, to build confidence is essentially to build trust, both in yourself and in the laws of nature. But like the chicken and the egg, which one comes first? You need experience to build confidence, and you need confidence to allow yourself to experience. I don't know the answer to the chicken-and-egg question, but for confidence, it turns out we all have it buried deep within us already, and the tool we use to develop it is courage.

In order to trust ourselves, we need to know what we're capable of, and to know what we're capable of, we probably need to test ourselves. And to trust how the world works, we can't rely on common knowledge, because common knowledge equals common results, and unfortunately, common results tend to be less than what we hope, dream, and expect of the world. We tend to be disappointed because we allow ourselves to be surprised, offended, and even victimized by the world simply doing what it does. As it turns out, we're trying to control the wrong shit. My hope is that in following my journey to work through my insecurities, it allows you to do the same for yourself as it did for me. When you become confident in your ability to develop your abilities, you'll become more effective in life, and hopefully, you'll pass on what you learn from your own journey to those who might need it for themselves. This book is my attempt to keep the relay going by passing the baton to you.

CHAPTER 1

WHO ARE YOU?

When I was young, I had no idea what I wanted to do when I grew up. I didn't know what my strengths were, and I didn't know where I fit into the world—probably just like most other kids. But I did know who I looked up to. I looked up to my dad, as most boys do. I looked up to a few of his friends as well. I looked up to my older brother and some of the musicians, actors, and athletes I watched and listened to. Each had certain traits that drew my admiration toward them. I couldn't have specifically articulated what they were at the time, but there was something about their presence that captivated my attention. Looking back, those attributes were often simple things, like a glowing smile. I assumed this meant they were generally happy, which is something worth being drawn to. They had a talent or skill—something useful they could offer to their society and for themselves. The fact that others also gave them credit suggested this was worthy of my curiosity. But the most common trait was that they all seemed comfortable in their own skin. I was drawn to them because they had what I wanted. When you're unsure of yourself and of life, you naturally feed off the self-assurance of people you trust. This is why we can be easily influenced by confident people. Their energy can make us feel safe.

As I grew older, my infatuation continued as I watched their lives unfold. Some of the people I admired proved my assumptions right, while others proved me dead wrong. They weren't all happy or as confident as they first appeared. Some of the skills I'd admired were even questionable—at least through the skeptical lens of a young adult whose idea of "good" had gradually escalated. I've realized that the flashes of confidence and happiness I'd seen were compartmental. I'd caught them in people when they were at their best. I discovered that someone who was happy in a social setting might go home and immediately remove the mask that covers a depression. The same person who is incredibly confident in the company of a certain group of people might be extraordinarily insecure in front of another. Humans naturally default to hierarchies, and confidence shines brighter at the top. Children, especially in past generations, were often at the bottom of hierarchies involving adults, so, naturally, they would see a disproportionate amount of confidence in the adults around them.

When we watch a professional athlete or musician performing, we're watching them in their element of genius. If they base their self-worth on that particular skill, it's no wonder they seem so confident. But how they feel about themselves when they are off the stage or the field, or after retirement, can be a completely different story. It turns out that confidence isn't consistent. Humans are more complex than we give ourselves credit for. It's confusing to try to make sense of conflicting traits, so we tend to accept what we see at face value as the only truth. But every one of us has one attribute that contradicts another. Everything you see in a person was developed with time and experience, and those experiences will cause personas to come out in different settings. If who we are is developed, does the credit (or the blame) lie in our genetics, or is it our environment that influences us?

THE COMPLEXITY OF HUMAN NATURE

On one hand, each of our respective ancestors passed on a piece of themselves to create their offspring, and their children did the same to their own children. Each generation passed a piece of their DNA on to the next one, over hundreds of thousands of years. What they ate, how they interacted socially, where they lived, and how they physically adapted to their environments all played a role in their development, and they passed this on through the generations, and eventually to us. We need only to look at our skin tones and bone structures to confirm the validity of genetics. The undeniable physical factors offer enough evidence of its role. With that in mind, surely genetics would play a large role in our personalities and, thus, our behavior. The seeds of a rose will never sprout a lily or a daisy. We know what it will become.

On the other hand, the complexity of humans is still beyond our own comprehension. Even in the argument for genetics, we can't discard the effects of our ancestors' environments. Surely each generation's unique challenges played a role in the *direction* of their development. The evolution of all living things is a slow adaptation to what is needed for survival. The behavior of each group within their circles influenced how they interacted with others. The food available in Africa is different than that available in China or in the frozen regions of North America. The physical requirements to hunt forced some tribes to run or to build strength and others to be patient. We literally built ourselves to be equipped for our unique environments and ways of life.

Water follows the natural laws of gravity. It flows down the path of least resistance as it carves out its course, constantly shaping itself with each obstacle it meets. Eventually, it joins a larger body of water and becomes what we see after time and continuous force. Humans, in a similar way, move through life, changing and adapting to their environments, and on the journey, they constantly become the person we see at this moment. Each day, we're a little different, as we evolve based on what is required of us—or at least what we believe is required.

Imagine this hypothetical circumstance: Two identical twins are separated at birth. One is raised in poverty within the ghettos of America, while the other is adopted and raised by upper-class parents in the richest part of the country. The two cultures could hardly be more different. One twin grows up in survival mode, never feeling safe. The other grows up in a life of comfort and security. The people are different, and the interactions are different. If the twins didn't meet each other until they were grown adults, how similar do you think they would be once they met?

My guess is that they might look the same and share some uncanny mannerisms. Perhaps they would share some of the same quirks—maybe the way they eat, smile, or scowl. But their stories about how the world works would be completely different, based on the environment in which they grew up. What was required from each to survive their individual world would be different; therefore, instinct would summon different skills, triggers, and defense mechanisms. One might dream more than the other, as he's given more space to do so, whereas the other isn't given enough space or time to think past surviving the day. If their aims are different, then so is the direction of their development. It's a fork in the road that continues to grow farther apart.

I'm not suggesting, however, that the child living a life of comfort had the advantage. His daily threats may have been a lack of love or militant parents who gave no room for personal expression. Perhaps they forcefully carved out a path for him that he didn't like. Maybe they too forcefully imposed expectations of who he should be and how he should think. This might trigger a rebellion, as we all need to come to be on our own terms. Though the threat isn't physical, he may be the one living in survival mode as he struggles to connect with his authentic self. The child growing up in the ghettos might be so dissatisfied with his circumstance that he becomes determined to create a different life for himself. Or maybe not. Life is too complex for us to predict, with certainty, who a person will become. We can play the odds game, but there are too many outliers to ignore. When does a negative influence us so much that we turn it into a positive, and when does a positive in the eyes of our society affect us so much that it becomes a handicap? How do we know who would become more and who would shrink as a result of the same challenged life? What we can be sure of is that both our environment and how we perceive it play a role in who we become.

THE THIRD FACTOR

The debate of nature versus nurture should end in a draw. They work together in making up the fabric of who we are. But there's a third factor that influences our development. This one is less obvious but arguably the most important, because it is the one we can learn to control. That factor is *choice*.

There are dormant forces within each of us. We have skills, thoughts, and ideas that are undeveloped. We have values and virtues that are cultivated each day by our choices and our efforts. But the less aware we are that we're doing it, the less power we have over its direction. Each day that we go about our life without a conscious intention is another day that we default to genetic tendencies and environmental circumstances. We relinquish the power to choose and ultimately become victims of chance. If this is the case, we can only hope that we got lucky and landed in an environment that influences productive thought and positive behavior. If we're relying on genetics, we can only hope that our ancestors put more effort than we did into their own development. If they worked hard to develop the best in themselves, they might have gifted us a head start over our peers. The reality is that we haven't all hit the genetic and environmental lottery. Even if our ancestors did their best to develop what was needed, it was intended for their own success in their own time. Those qualities you inherited might well equip you to perform exceptionally well in a world that you don't live in.

As we develop ourselves, we look to others who seem to be ahead on the trail for inspiration. It's not always positive, and as we learn how the world works and how people work within the world, we might realize that how others appear may simply be an illusion. We aren't creative enough to work with a completely blank canvas, and so the qualities and mannerisms of others still influence us. Sometimes it's enough to spark the development of qualities we admire in others within ourselves. But oftentimes, we become discouraged because we don't think those qualities we admire in others can be found within us. Outside inspiration certainly serves a useful purpose, but perhaps it's not *them* we want to become (or *not* become, if we're inspired by dissatisfaction). Perhaps studying others is simply a tool to help us discover our personal values. If we observe the results that others produce by their behavior, we learn a little more about ourselves. When we pay attention to the values and principles that guide their behavior, we can use them to properly align our own personal compasses. Both success and failure leave clues, and we can use them to point us in the direction of who we truly want to become.

CHAPTER 2

VALUES

If I were to ask you who you are, how would you respond? Would you tell me what you do for work? Or maybe what you do for fun? Would you tell me about your emotional tendencies—that you're "a happy person" or "a realist"—or would you tell me about your family, your friends, and your hobbies? These might truly shed a light on what your life is like, but what if all those circumstances changed? If we're to look deeper at our core, the stuff that won't change when our outside circumstances do, we will eventually find clarity in what we truly care about. No matter what changes on the outside, when everything else is stripped away, what is left is who you truly are. These are your core values. They are the root of all your choices and the source of your development.

When confronted with the difficult choices that life inevitably and frequently offers, how do we know that we're making the right ones? We need only to reflect on our core values in order to find the right answer—the one that comes from our authentic selves. What we care about determines what we become. But we don't do this automatically. When you aren't happy with who you are, that might be your conscience telling you that your choices are out of alignment with your values. These choices may be small and subtle, but small and subtle compounds, becoming ever more significant over time. Though we aren't taught to pay attention, deep down, we all hear that little voice inside of us. Sometimes it's subtle, and sometimes it isn't. If it doesn't speak to us through words inside our heads, it speaks through our bodies. Our physiology changes when something feels wrong compared to when something feels right. The reason we often ignore it is simple: self-reflection requires a lot of our energy, and the farther we've strayed from our authentic self, the more painful it can become.

To embrace that voice is to become conscious. It is being aware of our deepest self while simultaneously being aware of how we are living on the outside. The self we project to the world must be authentic to the self we truly are on the inside.

This requires effort and energy. We're constantly battling between our surface desires and our deeper ones, between our immediate wants and our future goals. The path of least resistance is to appease the immediate, because it is louder and the results come right now. Besides, it's much easier just to enjoy life as it comes. But the most successful people in life are the ones who make present decisions based on longer-term visions. They see farther out into the future and question their "in the moment" desires before choosing whether to succumb or not. They understand which choices today serve their ultimate goals, despite whether they satisfy their immediate "needs," and assess whether satisfying their present self is worth the trade for what their future self desires. This is self-mastery—the ability to consciously choose your actions (and reactions) that serve the more permanent "you." It is essential to living authentically and building true self-confidence.

THE MOST RELIABLE SOURCE OF TRUST

If another person in your life were to act in a way that compromised your well-being, how much would you trust him? Even if the actions weren't deliberate or intended to be malicious, you could not give him your full confidence because you would realize that you must protect your own welfare. With that said, if your present self were to act in a way that compromised the well-being of your future self, how could you ever be truly self-confident? Confidence is trust. It is the ability to rely on someone or something. Since life can throw a million circumstances at you, you must be able to depend on yourself to make good decisions for your future self. We can have faith that things turn out as they are meant to, but that isn't synonymous with trust. We can trust other people when we know they are good. But everyone is fighting their own battles, and even those with the utmost integrity can let us down if we catch them in the wrong moment. Therefore, the most reliable source of trust—of confidence—must be in yourself.

How do you build trust in yourself? Make the small choices that align with your values, and don't be hard on yourself when you slip. Forgive yourself and get right back on track. You'll have plenty more choices to make today, tomorrow, and the next day. As you improve on making the small choices that align with your values, your integrity grows stronger, and momentum shifts in your favor. Small choices become a default that requires less energy. They no longer feel like choices. Then, inevitably, you'll be tested with more difficult choices, and the same concept holds. Remind yourself to make the ones that align with your values, and again, don't be hard on yourself if you slip. You'll have the opportunity to make it right more often than you think. As you continue to do this, you will build trust in your ability to create a better environment for your future self. Over time, you'll become less preoccupied with what happens in your outer world, because you will trust yourself to properly handle any situation. As you build up your future rather than tearing it down in the service of your present desires, you're also building up the relationship between your present self, your future self, and eventually, your past self. This is self-confidence. This is self-assurance. This is self-love.

THE COYOTE AND THE CHOCOLATE CHIP COOKIE

I know what you're thinking. *Yeah, but how the fuck are we supposed to be happy now? Aren't we taught that to be truly happy is to live in the present moment? If all our choices are meant to serve our future selves, does that mean we sacrifice everything now for something later? What if that something never even happens?*

Our immediate desires are generally instinctive. They are animalistic. This serves animals well because their instincts serve their goals. Coyote sees rabbit; coyote hunts rabbit. If he's successful, he gets to eat and live another day. But the coyote should be thankful he doesn't have to deal with chocolate chip cookies. When the coyote eats his rabbit, he's getting the nutrients he needs. When he hunts, he keeps himself fit, sharp, and strong so he can continue to outsmart or outrun his prey; thus, he's capable of surviving another day. But what if the coyote had access to an endless supply of cookies, as we do? He wouldn't have to chase them, and he wouldn't have to work for them. It might feel like heaven at first. All the new flavors, the sweetness, and the incredible gooey texture. That poor coyote has no idea what he's missing out on, because life is all about the simple pleasures, right? Wrong.

The coyote has never had to practice self-control. When he was chasing rabbits, it was only time to stop eating when there was nothing left. If cookies were available to him, would he know when to stop? How would he know what nutrients serve his fitness and survival? Maybe he might get wise and just have some for a little treat after he catches his rabbit for the day. Yes, a reward for a good day's work. Life is short. Why not have the cookie? If the universe didn't want him to have cookies, why would they be available to him?

Thankfully, the coyote lives a simpler life. His goal is survival, and every day his actions align with who he is: a coyote. But animals don't need to find themselves. They're not on the same evolutionary path, and therefore, they don't need to create themselves. They don't need to consider their values. That's all sorted out, and we don't judge them for being what they are. Coyotes don't have to worry about the consequences of their actions because their environment sets the entire playing field for them. Even considering urban invasion, their lives and goals haven't changed over thousands of years.

Humans, on the other hand, have quite literally created the world we live in, and we continue to evolve it for ourselves. Therefore, we must constantly adapt to function within a changing world. Our survival depends on it. Though not physically as apparent as it once was, it is our *emotional* survival that is tested, and when we make poor choices, the pain can be unbearable. We have hundreds, if not thousands, of choices to make each day. What should I wear? When should I go to sleep? What should I do for work? What's the best way to train my employee? Should I get married? Does it matter what my parents think? Should I have kids? Should I yell to get what I want? Should I treat other ethnicities better? Should I drop what I'm doing and help the needy? Should I take a trip? Will I get sick? What should I take if I do? Can I trust this person? What is that person thinking? Are we destroying our own planet? Should we have heavier gun laws? Should we colonize Mars? Is it okay to spank my children? Why can't I control myself when I'm drinking? Why do I feel unhappy? I could keep going forever.

Life is complex because of endless choices. It's hard to know what's right and wrong when there are so many variables at play, when so many people have such varied opinions, and when some embrace and advocate for the harder questions, while others resist them. Just thinking about it can be overwhelming. Though it was often more brutal, our ancestors lived a much simpler life, one more similar to wild animals. A focus on physical survival didn't leave much room for complexities. As we evolved, we learned to build constructs that would shield us from past challenges, but with the elimination of past dangers, our primal instincts remained with us. What served us in the past now hurts us if we don't attempt to control it.

STEERING EVOLUTION

The tribes of the past didn't need to worry about how they made other tribes feel. They were separate, and if one was a threat to the other, they defaulted to ensuring their own survival without overthinking it. If the death of another was required for their survival, that was okay. It was brutal, but it was simple.

Before we industrialized our food supply, our ancestors didn't need to worry about eating artificial and genetically modified foods, because they didn't exist. We created our food system to ameliorate our quality of life, and it worked to some degree. But a society that creates a new system comes from the old system. When a new system is created to solve an old problem, it inadvertently creates a new problem in its place. Now the new solution must come from a different level of thinking, a deeper level than the one that created the problem in the first place. This is the beauty of our evolving society. Though its complexity can leave us confused, frustrated, and anxious at times, it's also quite beautiful when you step back and observe what is really happening. We're constantly becoming. As we live in a time where we're made more aware of our social problems, we tend to think the world is getting worse. We thought racism was almost gone, and then we realized it continues to persist. We thought equality was balancing out, and then we realized we're not all treated equally. We thought our quality of life was improving, and then it felt like everything was getting worse.

The truth is that life is improving! With progress, we uncover new challenges, we solve them, and new ones unfold. To solve the next problem on the outside, we need to go deep inside yet again. The harder the challenge, the deeper we must go, and with each event, we uncover more of who we are. As we uncover this, we find more of ourselves that we need to work on. This constant unfolding of life is what we call evolution.

Expect the unexpected. If we know that every solution uncovers a new problem, instead of being surprised or even offended by it, we can embrace and recognize it as our next opportunity to grow. This is the constant flow of life, and when you resist it, you're missing the point. You're no longer playing the game. You'll constantly feel like you're swimming against the current, as if the world is conspiring against your every move. Conversely, once you accept your challenges, your story completely changes. It's as if you suddenly turned around, hopped on a life raft, and are simply floating along with the current. Your direction now follows the flow of life, and the resistance dissipates into thin air.

As these new problems unfold, it still isn't easy. With every challenge, we're faced with a choice, and because it's often a new experience, we can't reference that experience from events in our past. We need, instead, to look to our core values. They are the root of our deepest needs and desires. How we choose to react to circumstances determines which part of ourselves we develop. It's another fiber in who we're becoming. When we know what we stand for and what is ultimately important to us, we can act with confidence. We know where to start, and we can feel good about it, because our core values provide the answers to whom we want to become and what we're really trying to accomplish.

Anytime you're faced with a difficult choice, you find your answer when you go back to what you stand for. When you omit this step, you instead wrestle with what's satisfying now versus what would ultimately bring the best results. Remember, you're not a coyote. He doesn't need to wrestle with the complexity of these questions.

When we're clear on our values, our anxieties and stresses dissipate, because we know that when our choices are in alignment with our values, we're making the right decisions—the ones that steer our evolution in the right direction. We might still question ourselves, but when we do, it's rooted in love and excitement for what might come rather than out of fear of getting things we don't want. This is how we can be present while still thinking of the future. When we know we're making choices in the present that create a better future, how could we not be happy in that moment? There's nothing to worry about because we know that, no matter what life throws at us, we'll figure out what to do. We trust that, one way or another, we're going to be okay. Since we've embraced the idea that life is supposed to bring challenges, we stop wishing for it to be easy, and we start looking forward to what's coming next.

THE VIRUS OF THOUGHT

In the previous section, I referenced societal and political issues and crossed into personal solutions. If that confused you, let me explain. Each of us makes up our society. It's easy to dismiss our individual importance, as if we disappear in the sea of loud voices and large groups. But, like the fibers from your shirt, each one weaves into the next to make up its whole. Macroscopic issues, those that affect societies, are simply a collection of microscopic issues—individual belief systems. Each of our beliefs is handed down from past generations, and they evolve with time. More directly, each person acts as a fuel cell that keeps their beliefs alive and shared among society. Thoughts and ideas spread the same way viruses do. As they trigger our emotional responses, they pass from one human to the next, and each person's "immune system" determines whether they become infected with the new ideas, regardless of whether they are good or bad. Those thoughts and ideas spread from one person to others, and, like the heat from a wildfire, the stronger the issue, the faster it catches. At some point, those ideas will be met with resistance—the opposite frame of reference, which may grow just as strong.

This is the reality of life. It is what connects us just as much as it separates us. It can be a beautiful thing, and it can be an awful thing. Each of us is a product of our environment. The more we hear of one opinion or one ideal, the more likely we are to absorb it. The more people accept it as their true story, the stronger it gets. It's going to happen, whether we're conscious of it or not, but when we *are* conscious of it, we have more power to choose its direction. When you know at your core what matters to you, and when you're aware of what opinions, thoughts, and ideals are crowding your space, you can begin to choose more freely which to accept as your own. Just like your body's immune system, your conscience can fight what doesn't serve you.

DOES IT SERVE YOU?

Immune systems aren't perfect. If you don't want to

catch a cold, stay away from your sick friends until they recover. Expose yourself to a virus long enough and even the strongest immune system will eventually wear down and become defeated. With this in mind, what does your everyday environment look like? The friends you spend time with, the news you watch, and the posts on your social media feed will never be perfect, but if you can, you may want to limit or eliminate the ones that don't serve you. Social media is the best example of how easily we become influenced. When your friends constantly post their theories of how the world is going to shit, or how everyone is going crazy, or that everything is going wrong for them, it might serve you better to hit the snooze button on their posts. If you pay attention to how you feel after leaving a conversation or watching a bit of news, and you feel drained rather than energized, you might consider avoiding those environments when you can.

The stronger frame always wins. When you truly understand yourself, and when you know what you stand for, you can trust yourself. You now become the one who infects other people. Energy is contagious in either direction. Mahatma Gandhi's brilliant advice to "be the change you wish to see in the world" was meant in this way. Who you are being affects everyone around you, just as everyone else's "being" will affect you. When your frame is powerful enough (and it always eventually is), it creates a ripple effect and eventually renders you responsible for how your world is shaped. Make sure you're affecting things in the direction you would like to see. Before you hit send on that Facebook post, make sure it's something worth putting out. Before you complain about a situation to your friends, ask yourself what you're really trying to accomplish. Are you looking for sympathy, or are you looking to solve a problem? Here's a good way to test yourself: ask, *If everyone acted this way, would the world become better or worse?* Or ask yourself, *If I did this all the time, would it improve my life, or would it worsen it?* Choose carefully—our actions slowly become us, and we aren't the only ones affected. Everyone is.

CHAPTER 3

EGO

———

If you start to believe that you're as important as I'm suggesting, will you become like all the obnoxious people you identify in your life with an inflated ego? Will you become just like the celebrities and the extroverted success stories who make a point to ensure that the world knows how important they are? Only if you miss the point.

Every one of us has an ego. Whether you're shy and reserved or loud and boisterous, whether you're self-absorbed or extremely giving, whether you're a jerk or incredibly kind, you have an ego. Your ego is simply the awareness of *you*. It allows you to recognize yourself as an individual person who makes up this world. Without it, you couldn't survive. If your ancestors hadn't been aware of their singularity, they wouldn't have run from the saber-toothed tiger that preyed on them. They would have stayed in place and given themselves to the tiger who needed to eat, completely indifferent to their personal survival, because they wouldn't have seen themselves as separate from anything of the world, including the tiger. As for the modern human, we wouldn't look both ways before we cross the street, nor would we defend ourselves in an attack from predators. Death in our world happens each moment of each day, just as new life does. Therefore, if you only saw yourself as one with the universe, you would hold no regard for your own life, because universal life never ends. Without ego, our world would never have become what it is today. We've villainized the word over the past few generations, embracing the idea that if we see ourselves as good people, we don't have an ego, and only "they" do. The irony of that thought is quite entertaining when you think about it. If there is such a thing as "they," that means there is an "I" or a "we," which is the manifestation of your ego. You can't get away from it!

TROUBLE IN PARADISE

In 2008, I was entering my second year of working in real estate, and my business was starting to take off. At only twenty-four years old, I married my wife, Avarey, and within three years, we had two perfect, healthy boys, Owen and Jaxson. By my mid-twenties, I was living the good life. I had the big home in suburbia, two SUVs, two kids, two dogs, two houses, a boat, an RV, and a great business. It was more than I ever expected.

I attributed my newfound success to self-education. It started with sales CDs, then expanded to books, business coaching, and podcasts. I spent the majority of my free time consuming content related to business, money, and success. Eventually, my interests were steered toward improving life in general. Most of the content argued that building success in all areas of life generally leads to a better business. After all, the engine of a car runs much better when it's firing on all cylinders. I wasn't simply learning tactics to make more money. I was learning to live a better life, and I got really excited about it because I could see the results unfolding. Though I had challenges, I was able to work through them, and I was already living a better life than I'd ever imagined. (Truth be told, I hadn't imagined anything spectacular.)

All through this journey, Avarey didn't care for the books, the podcasts, and the coaching. Not for herself, anyway. She was supportive of my passion and thankful for the results that it brought to our family, but self-improvement was my thing, not hers.

Flash forward to 2015. I had become one of the top real estate agents in the city. My self-education was stronger than ever as I continued reading great books, business coaching, and masterminding with several powerful groups. I had moved my family into the neighborhood I dreamed of when I was a kid, right down the street from where my wealthy childhood friends lived. I bought a brand-new Porsche, and I was taking my family on amazing vacations multiple times each year. I was in the best shape I'd ever been—both physically and emotionally. My finances were looking good, and I'd built a real estate team with an incredible culture. It was seemingly perfect, yet something was still missing.

My marriage wasn't where I wanted it to be. Avarey has always been a kind person, but when you have two crazy toddler boys, moms are in a difficult place. There is no energy left at the end of the day. Just as most fathers during this time, I didn't feel important. I didn't feel the love I needed, and I started to resent my wife. I felt that we had grown apart as I was on my journey of personal growth. I hated that, in our downtime, I was reading books and setting big life goals, while she was watching *The Bachelor* and reading celebrity magazines. Being the kind of person who doesn't keep things to myself, I was verbal about it. From my perspective, she didn't seem interested in changing, and I couldn't force her to be someone she wasn't.

My conclusion was that I had married too young. I had married before I knew who I was and who she was, so I decided I wanted out. When I told Avarey that I wasn't happy and that I wanted to leave, she took it seriously. She didn't want it to end, and, to her credit, she forced herself to make efforts in the areas that bugged me. She tried to power her way through a book that I had put on her nightstand many years prior. The book was *The 7 Habits of Highly Effective People* by Stephen Covey.

In my mind, it was too late. Her effort was only there because it had to be. My plan to leave was made, and I was on my way out. Yet something kept me from moving forward. If there's anything I've learned from my business that I could use in my relationship, it was that success is not simply a result of hard work. It comes from digging deep and finding that next gear that you never knew you had. It comes from both committing to the process and practicing *excellence*. Deep down, I knew that if I gave up before giving a legitimate 100 percent effort to our marriage, I would regret it for the rest of my life. I wasn't done trying, and so I decided to stay.

Through the difficulty, our relationship wasn't one of conflict and fighting. It was more one of pain and lethargy. The strength of emotions was so high that time seemed to stand still, and every moment was almost surreal. It was like living inside of a bad dream.

However, there was still some mutual respect between the two of us. One day, Avarey was lying across the foot of the bed with her *7 Habits* book opened to the section that included a chart that helps depict a person's center. It explained that people view the world from different paradigms. We each view our worlds from a lens that is centered from a different point of view—ultimately from who or what is most important to you. For some, the world revolves around their children; for others, it revolves around their work, or church, or even pleasure, and there are nine or ten more examples of different centers. Knowing that I love this book, Avarey asked me to look at the chart and figure out where my own center was. I appeased her and read through each one, scanning through each explanation until I could identify my own center. When I got to the one that most felt like mine, I stopped dead in my tracks. It felt like I had just hit a brick wall going one hundred miles per hour. As I gathered myself to figure out what had just happened, a better version of myself appeared to help me up, but instead of consoling me, he bitch-slapped me in the face and said, "Wake up, motherfucker!" I was *self-centered*.

When I could only view the world through my own lens, I was so caught up in my personal story that I was oblivious to how my behavior could be the very thing that obstructed me from having what I was after—a great marriage. This was a revelation.

I thought I was a good person. I was sincere, honest, and hardworking, and I cared immensely about others. I wanted the absolute best for my family, my clients, my colleagues, and my friends. I constantly received feedback from others that they saw me in the same way. After all, their feedback was how I built my self-image (and thus my self-esteem). So how was it that I could be both giving and self-centered? In my mind, self-centered people are bad people. They don't contribute good things to society, and they don't care about others. Shattering my view of who I am was painful. How could I be something without ever realizing it?

THE HIERARCHY OF HUMAN NEEDS

When you embrace your ego rather than rejecting it, you start to become aware of when it controls your decisions. Its primary function is to ensure your survival, and it serves you well to engage it. The more you're focused on survival, the stronger your ego controls your thoughts and actions.

Because you must meet your primary needs before you have the capacity to care about much else, you will feel more separated from the world. When you feel separate and alone, your ego is telling you that you need to give yourself attention. Don't ignore that message—it's there to help you. But, at the same time, don't let it fool you into thinking that excluding others or pushing them away is the answer to your personal solution.

Abraham Maslow developed a hierarchy of human needs that explains this perfectly.

Maslow's Hierarchy of Needs

Self-
Actualization
Desire to be the
most that one can be

Esteem
Respect, Freedom, Strength,
Self-Esteem, Status, Recognition

Love & Belonging
Family, Friendship, Intimacy,
Sense of connection

Safety Needs
Security, Employment, Resources, Health, Property

Physiological Needs
Food, Water, Air, Shelter, Sleep, Reproduction

Our primary needs start at the bottom, and once we feel safe that need has been met, our attention moves up to the next tier, as we slowly relax our self-focus and enlighten ourselves to the larger picture. As we move up through the hierarchy of needs, we begin to feel more connected to our world and to the rest of humanity. Our goals become inclusive rather than exclusive.

The keyword in personal development is "personal." It is important to work on ourselves, and there is a time to focus deeply on yourself. This should remain constant throughout your life, regardless of where you're at in Maslow's hierarchy of needs. Because, after all, if we want to contribute to others, we are much more effective when we're the best version of ourselves. And we don't become our best without self-focus and reflection. The challenge, however, is that the pattern of our growth must evolve, and if we're to move up the hierarchy, we must force ourselves to see ourselves and our situations through a different lens.

When in an airplane, the flight attendants give us their pre-takeoff instructions. The most notable of these is that in case of an emergency, an oxygen mask will pop out in front of you. You must first place the oxygen mask over yourself before you help even your own children place theirs. At face value, it seems selfish to save yourself before your own children, doesn't it? It's quite the opposite, actually. If you stop breathing, you're in no condition to help them or anyone else. Everyone loses. The rest of life works the same way.

For much of my childhood, I was homeschooled and therefore had a lot of time to spend with myself. I was also introverted and rebellious. I watched my family broken apart by drug addiction and, as a result, moved out of my parents' house at fourteen years old. I continued to attend school and even enrolled in night classes, all while working full-time. Focusing on myself for survival was necessary. My world today wouldn't exist if I hadn't focused on myself as intensely as I did, and it worked. My ego is responsible not just for my survival but also for much of my success. But fifteen years later, it had served its purpose. My basic needs were met and my oxygen mask was already on, yet instead of looking over to see if anyone else needed help putting theirs on, I kept focusing on making sure mine stayed intact. Without conscious thought, I still allowed my survival instincts to narrate my story. I feared that if I took my attention away from myself for even a moment, everything I had built might crumble. My ego had served me incredibly well, and now I finally caught a glimpse of how it had gone too far.

Though I had read that section of *7 Habits* before, I wasn't ready for the message the first time. We can read the same words and receive their message completely differently based on what we have happening in our lives (this is the story-filter we all use). This message was past due, and I finally realized it was time to change my paradigm. The only way to build the family life I wanted wasn't to change the people in it; it was to change how I fit myself into the family I already had, and that was going to be a challenge. It required growth. It required intention, and, in a weird way, it required courage. If I wanted to authentically become someone I wasn't being, I needed to let go of my fear that relaxing my self-focus equated to losing my edge on the path to success. At the time, that felt like a death sentence. There was no way I'd be doomed to struggling the way I had as a kid, and the way my parents had in my youth. I simply would never go back to that, at any cost. I knew that if I wanted to save my marriage, I needed to challenge my paradigm of how to achieve success, because my current strategy had reached a stalemate. It was game over *unless* I no longer accepted the notion that one area of success had to come at the sacrifice of another.

INCLUSIVE INTENTIONS

When we satisfy our basic needs of survival, our instincts recognize that ego served us well. A self-focus gets us fed, it keeps our bodies healthy, and it is essential in developing life skills. It serves us especially well when outside help is limited and we have to fight for it ourselves. When we think of those people who achieve great success in their lives and who appear to have come from nothing, defying the odds to accomplish big things in life, we realize their spark often came from tremendous personal pain. Self-focus is a necessity for survival, but once your more basic needs are met, you will crave deeper meaning. You'll be more aware of needing connection and love from others, and if you're fortunate enough to recognize you already have that, but you still feel something is missing, you might realize that you need to build a higher regard for yourself. If you're blessed enough to feel those needs are met, and yet you still feel something is missing, you might then realize that everything you've learned in your life—all the challenges, the wins, and the learning experiences—the gifts you've developed in yourself, are meant to be shared with others. This is your contribution to the world. The more you open yourself up to sharing your best self—your true authentic self—the more you'll realize your own significance.

That journey is for everyone, not just a select few. Think of the person who's had the greatest impact on you. I bet it's someone you know personally. And I bet the quality of the person who was life-changing for you might seem insignificant, and maybe even ordinary, to someone else. It might be something as small as them demonstrating how to work hard. Maybe your dad was a carpenter who brought passion to his craft and showed you never to cut corners, even when no one can see the work. If that resonated and you adapted that work ethic not just to woodworking but to other areas of life, I bet it served you well and helped you accomplish things you couldn't have otherwise. That is *impact*. However, if your dad hadn't taken the time to share that value with you, how different would things have turned out? Maybe a stranger in a sales transaction blew you away by clearly demonstrating that she cared more about you than she did about her sale or paycheck. Maybe you'd never had that experience before, and it inspired you to put a customer first just once. And maybe you recognized how safe your customer felt when you did that, just as you did when you were in their shoes, so you decided that's how you'd work all the time. Then, as a result, you continued to attract more success. If you were changed by one small interaction with another, is it possible you've affected another person the same way as well? Never underestimate the ripple effect of your actions.

Those positive contributions come easier when we're in a higher state. But rarely does anyone sit permanently in any specific tier of Maslow's hierarchy. As life brings constant change, we might shift between basic and higher needs. When something seems to be slipping away from us, we begin to feel threatened, and thus, our ego engages in an effort to protect us. It becomes more difficult to care about contributing to others. Like the tides of the ocean, our varying circumstances require different effort and attention. When we're in survival mode, we're naturally going to focus more on ourselves. When we do, we need to make sure that we don't have the inverse effect on others. For, as powerful as positive contribution is, negative contribution has the same ripple effect, and often it can cause damage at a much faster rate. A city can take decades or even centuries to build bridges, skyscrapers, houses, roads, and art. And in one moment, a tsunami, a hurricane, or a tornado can knock it all down. Its destructive effect is disproportionate to the time and effort invested in its construction.

The same holds true for our contribution to the world. That salesperson who changed your life by sacrificing her needs for yours might be in the middle of a bad divorce, and now she's in financial trouble. She's not herself because her whole being feels threatened. Maybe on her next transaction, she now needs the money and takes advantage of her next customer, utilizing her sales skills to satisfy her own interests. She finds a way to justify her actions by telling herself that sales is her job, and therefore she can't be judged for doing what she's paid to do. But her customer feels it. He feels remorse after his purchase because he bought the wrong product. Maybe that customer ends up in a sales role himself. He sees that the tactic clearly worked on him, so this becomes his paradigm for success in sales. And so, over time, each of those salespeople affects each of their customers, and this becomes the expectation for the sales profession. In a short period of time, everyone has their guard up, and they expect that no one has their best interests at heart. They certainly don't refer their friends and family to that salesperson either. Therefore, he must continuously work to find new customers to take advantage of, and his job becomes harder. Everyone loses.

SACRIFICING VALUES

This is the danger of ego. Our self-focus must never be at the sacrifice of others. When our instinct says to do what it takes to survive, we have to question objectively whether the issue at hand is a matter of true survival. Even when life seems to be slipping away from us, we have to be real with ourselves and assess where we're really at in our situation. Then, when we have the opportunity to gain, we must ask ourselves if our gain will be made by sacrificing someone else's well-being and if that's really worth it. We should question whether it is really a gain in the end or if it just feels that way in the moment. When you start to contradict your values in an effort to survive, your journey back to the top of the hierarchy of needs will be compromised. You'll feel as though the world is conspiring to keep you down, and it becomes a "you versus them" game rather than a "me helping the world and the world helping me" game. It might serve you for a while. You'll probably succeed quickly in getting your basic needs met, but you will struggle to find any love and connection. You will struggle to build your true self-esteem and confidence because your trust in your ability to live your own core values will fade with each compromise you make.

Your instinct, whether conscious or subconscious, might be that, if you're in survival mode, you can focus on being a better person to others once you have the capacity to do so. This rationale undoubtedly makes the start of the journey easier, but in the long run, it makes the journey to the top more difficult. To be more frank, it becomes next to impossible. The key to getting to the top of the hierarchy is to be the person who would already be up there, even when you're at the bottom. If you choose to be that person, you'll take different actions, and our actions ultimately attract what we get in life. If that salesperson who is going through hell at home were to step back and assess her situation, she would understand that, though her family is gone, as is the wealth she accrued, she still has a choice about who she ultimately wants to be. But she chooses that now, in the present, not later, when she feels better. If she remembers who she was being when everything was going great and channels that now, she might choose a different path, despite how unnatural it feels while she's in pain. The sacrifice of putting her customer's needs before her own is now even more difficult, but she can choose that path. She may not feel it immediately, but over time, and directly as a result of her better intentions, she attracts more good things into her life. She positively influences more people and attracts more good people into her life. She eventually finds herself back at the top of that hierarchy of needs, but this time she's even stronger because her character was tested harder than it was the first time. As a consequence, doing the right thing becomes natural and almost effortless.

THE OPPORTUNITY

If this person had chosen to focus on getting what she needed in the moment rather than on being who she wanted to ultimately be, how different do you think her life would have turned out? How different do you think things would be for the people she interacted with? Never underestimate the power of who you're being within every given moment. No matter what you're going through, you can bet that most others around you have their own challenges. When they are in a state of preservation, and a stranger offers an act of genuine kindness, it can leave an impression that stays with them forever. When a stranger acts in a selfish way, that might also leave an impression that stays forever. Which impression would you prefer to be responsible for, and which would help build your own esteem?

With this said, when your character is tested, and you ultimately make the choice to become your best self, it is difficult not to build confidence. When you know who you want to be, each action you take that aligns with that person compounds, and you build trust in yourself. It doesn't mean you always get it right, but if you continue to check in and realign, it leads to more self-trust. After a few instances of realignment, you realize your ability to always come back when you stray away. So don't be hard on yourself when you screw up. You probably will, because testing is part of the process. Each time you mess up, there's an opportunity to make it right. The harder it is to do that, the bigger the opportunity to build your character, and thus to build your confidence.

CHAPTER 4

DISCIPLINE AND INTEGRITY

When you drive your car across a bridge, how often do you wonder if it will crumble and fall while you're on it? The media loves to report on disasters, yet we hardly see news of catastrophic bridge failures. It's really quite amazing how little we need to concern ourselves with. Bridges can suspend over eleven hundred feet in the air, the tallest being the Aizhai bridge in China. They can span for miles and miles over water, the longest being the Lake Pontchartrain Causeway in Louisiana, at more than twenty-three miles. They are built over water that is hundreds of feet deep, and they must be built to withstand all of nature's harsh and unpredictable elements. They're not all straight, either, as many can bend and twist. Some can even separate and lift to allow ships to pass through. They do all this while bearing the load of millions of tons of steel moving at high speeds each and every day, for decades upon decades. We've grown so accustomed to bridges that most of us never fear anything bad happening as we cross one. We trust that it will do its job without fail, each and every time.

When a bridge is built, the engineering team takes it very seriously. They have to think through all the possible breaking points, the load, and all the elements that will test it over time. They spend ample time designing it to withstand these elements, and they test it numerous times to ensure its *integrity*. Because they developed a system, and we trust the care that has been put into it, we're afforded the luxury of not having to think about its safety. Though our lives depend on a bridge working, we can focus on other areas of our lives that need attention. They've got us covered.

The more consistent an occurrence, the more we can rely on it. We depend on the sun to come up in the morning and to go down at night. We rely on the earth to provide us with oxygen and nutrients. Since that comes to us consistently, we don't have to think or worry about whether that crucial need will be fulfilled. If it's as consistent as the sun rising each morning, or a bridge allowing us safe passage, we might even forget about it altogether. Trust allows us to let go and to focus on our other needs. When we have a car, we rely on it to get us to where we want to go, whenever we want to get there. If it starts to give us problems, that will get our attention. If the problems continue, we might even begin resenting it, and we'll figure out how to replace it, because we don't want to have to wonder if today is the day that it lets us down.

HUMAN INTEGRITY

Humans work the same way. As complex as manmade structures like bridges and cars can be, we are significantly more intricate. As a result, we're less consistent, and we know that we cannot depend on every person to do the right thing every time. Each person has their own battles—their own trials and tests. Like the engineer testing a bridge for its integrity, life tests each of us for ours. It looks for our stress cracks. Life is overwhelming when we think of all the things that can go wrong. For as many things that are consistent in this world, there's an equal or greater amount of inconsistencies. When we accept what is out of our control, it becomes clear that our greatest source of trust is within ourselves. Your ability to do the right thing regardless of the load you are put under—that is your *integrity*.

When someone lets you down, does your level of trust increase, stay the same, or decrease? For some, the shock of being let down might be devastating enough to erode your trust forever. Others might easily forgive, being willing to give that person another chance. But subtle as it might be, your bond of trust still suffered a fracture that will have to be earned back over time. If they open up to you by sharing their vulnerability and giving you a true glimpse of who they are, you might empathize well enough to allow that wound to heal, as long as their actions moving forward are consistent and transparent. However, most importantly, they have to *own* their mistake, leaving no blame on circumstances or other people. If they don't, they are revealing the crack in their own integrity. If the blame comes from outside of themselves, they are essentially revealing that they will do it again because they won't have control over their actions when that same situation happens to them again. Remember, a bridge never blames the elements if it fails. All that matters is the result. The engineer, then, isn't attached to what the bridge is or isn't. He modifies his design to withstand what might come its way. For people, this isn't necessarily to suggest that you should remove the person who broke your trust from your life. Recognize their humanity with empathy, because we all have a breaking point, but take note so you're not surprised the next time there is a compromise.

With this in mind, what happens when you let yourself down? This principle of trust toward others holds the same truth in your relationship with yourself. As you demonstrate acts of integrity toward yourself (the things you do when no one else is looking or when you know that no one will find out), your character strengthens. As you do this with the small things in life, you are building your muscles of integrity for the more challenging tests that will inevitably come. But we won't always *feel* like doing the right thing. It's difficult sometimes, especially for those of us who tend to operate at a highly emotional level. Our behavior rides the waves of our emotions. If this is the case, hoping we're in the right mental space all the time is a flawed plan because it releases personal responsibility. Just as in the case of the integrity-compromised person in the previous example, if we blame our destructive behavior on how we feel, we're essentially revealing to ourselves the weakness of our own integrity.

Without care and awareness of this tendency, it can be a dangerous place to operate. Because I often *feel* like eating sugar. I often *feel* like yelling at the idiot who disagreed with me and telling him how I "really feel." I often don't *feel* like following through on my commitments when I'm tired. But when I act in opposition to what I know would ultimately serve me best, the irony of my initial intention is that I end up feeling worse than I did before. It drains my energy thinking about it, and thus my capacity to do the things I should or shouldn't do dissipates. This creates a downward spiral that grows harder to escape at each full cycle. The good news is that the same momentum holds true in the opposite direction. The momentum that builds up our integrity strengthens with each cycle, and living in alignment can become our default.

A TOOL TO BUILD INTEGRITY

The most useful tool we can use to strengthen our integrity is discipline. Synonymous with self-mastery, discipline is the ability to follow through on our choices, long after the state we felt when we made that choice has passed. Discipline means we continue to find ways to fulfill our commitments despite what the world and people throw at us. When we've thought through a decision that we know will enrich our lives, discipline leaves no room to renegotiate. Each battle we win at successfully doing what serves us over what is easy becomes another experience of our personal power. As we stack these experiences, we strengthen the trust we have in ourselves to take care of our future selves. It isn't easy, and that is precisely what we want because overcoming easy things is not how we build *confidence*. It is not the way we build strength.

If you don't think you're a disciplined person, I have good news. Every one of us has discipline, but it isn't something that just happens. When you see a disciplined person, rest assured that he put effort and intention into being that way. Discipline is a practice that must be developed. Just like any other character trait, and just like the muscles in your body, it is strengthened with time and effort. Start by simply making the choice *to* start. In your first-ever workout, you wouldn't load three hundred pounds on a bar and squat for twenty reps. (Or maybe you would, but you'd regret it!) You need to work your way up to that. Discipline works the same way. Start with something small. One thing you want to work on, and one thing only. If you try multiple new disciplines, you'll quickly grow tired, and that's a recipe for collapse. It's a terrible plan.

Choose one thing that matters to you most and tell yourself each day that you will follow through. Don't bend. If you allow yourself space to cheat, you will always need to summon the energy to wrestle with your own rules, and eventually, you will wear down. Discipline requires mental energy, which is a finite resource. We only have so much of it, and no matter how strong you are, you will eventually wear yourself down. Your goal is to work yourself to a point where you don't need to wrestle with saying yes or no. It becomes an automatic response.

Personally, I have no self-control over chocolate chip cookies. I fucking love them, and when I have one, I can't help but have another and another. I wrestled forever with placing a limit on how many I could have and when I could have them. I have very strong willpower, but eventually, it gets me. Deciding to quit eating chocolate chip cookies forever was the best decision I ever made. Now I've simply trained myself to think, *I don't eat that.* That's the end of the conversation in my head. I can move on to something else instead of thinking, *But it's delicious. One can't hurt. You work out hard so you can afford to have one or two.* I can justify all of those excuses, and one really won't kill me, but what slowly kills me is having to go back to spending mental energy on my diet. It's draining, and if I spend my energy on wrestling with desserts, I'm taking away from spending mental energy on other things, because I don't have an endless supply. I'm not suggesting that everyone should stop eating cookies, though. That's a personal choice for me. I don't like being owned by anything, and chocolate chip cookies had my number for too long. Not anymore!

Discipline sustained in one area over time becomes a habit. The famous Stoic Aristotle once said, "We are what we repeatedly do. Excellence, then, is not an act, but a habit." Our habits shape who we are, and they shape the trajectory of our lives. But habits are built. We create them either by defaulting to our environment or by discipline. If we default to our environment, we relinquish any personal power. But if we create habits with intention, we apply discipline, and over time it becomes our default way of life, no longer requiring the same energy it took to get started.

THE DISCIPLINE THAT EASES ALL OTHER DISCIPLINES

Discipline is hard. It requires energy, and as I keep mentioning, we don't have an infinite amount in one day. If you aren't sure which discipline you should start with, let me tell you. It's *sleep*. No matter how good you think you are at operating on low amounts of sleep, you're not better than you would be on the right amount. When we lack sleep, our judgment changes. Our minds aren't as sharp, so we don't think as clearly or as quickly. Our bodies are in survival mode. We crave bad foods, and we succumb to temptations more easily. We're less happy because we're too busy being grumpy. If we're less happy, we look for immediate solutions to fix that. Sugar and carbohydrates make great immediate solutions, but the immediate fix is a sacrifice to our future self. It creates a downward spiral, dissipating our energy and increasing our dependence.

When we're tired, it's hard to get ourselves into the right mental state. It's hard to spend time thinking about our future, about who we want to become, and about what we want to accomplish in the world. It robs us of creating meaning—a reason in our lives to even create discipline. When we're tired, we don't want to read great books, talk with interesting people, create things we don't need to create, and perform physical activities we don't need to perform. We want to do the easy stuff. We want to watch television, surf on Facebook, and eat a doughnut or two (or, in my case, chocolate chip cookies).

Conversely, when we're wide awake, we have the energy to dream, conspire, build, think deeply, exercise more, and meet with great people who inspire us. All of these activities create more energy. When we're excited about possibilities and we have enough energy to see them through, discipline becomes much easier. It's hard to start, but once you set your goals and you see and feel the benefits, you'll work your ass off to make sure you don't spiral back down the other way. Sleep is a constant test and will always require intention and a little discipline, but it's the discipline that eases all other disciplines.

There are too many books already written on the subject, so I won't touch on it more except to say this, borrowed from my mentor, Richard Robbins: "The discipline of sleep is not to wake up in the morning. It is to go to bed early at night." Do yourself a favor and try it for a month. You'll thank me later.

CHAPTER 5

THE GREAT CANADIAN DEATH RACE—DEVELOPING DISCIPLINE

———

In my teens and my early twenties, I had many vices. Nothing incredibly unusual, but they were there, none-theless, and I wasn't aware that they weren't serving me. I started smoking cigarettes at age twelve and was soon going through a full pack each day—and I loved it. It was a social thing, and in my mind, it's what separated the nerds and the goody-goodies from the cool people. (It was a different era—don't judge!) Once I gained my freedom, I loved to drink excessively and stay up late. I would go out with my friends at least four nights per week, running on three or four hours of sleep and going to work all day the next day, just to do it all over again. I also loved sugar and sweets. In high school, I was working as a cashier in a grocery store, and on my lunch breaks, I would buy either a doughnut or a roll of premade Pillsbury cookie dough to eat for lunch. It was a nice break from the peanut butter and jam sandwiches that I ate every other meal. Living on my own in high school, no one could tell me what I could or couldn't eat.

Though I was never obese, I certainly didn't feel good about how I looked. It always bugged me a little, but not enough to do anything about it. As I started dating my now wife, my habits improved slightly, but my metabolism was slowing as I entered my twenties. I didn't truly realize what I looked like until one day when a friend posted a photo of me and a few other friends at the beach. I had my shirt off with my hat on backward, a cigarette in one hand and a beer in the other. When I looked at the photo, I had to do a double take to make sure it was really me. I had fucking man-boobs! It was devastating. The image I had of myself was not what I saw in that picture.

That day, I decided I would never allow myself to look like that again. The choice was pure vanity, as I wasn't concerned about my health in my early twenties. I just wanted to look better. I wanted to be comfortable with my shirt off. I was already lifting weights, but without any professional guidance, it clearly wasn't working to make me look fit. So I started running. The first time I tried, I made it about two blocks before I had to slow down and walk. I was already in pain and out of breath. What the fuck? I certainly wasn't motivated to keep doing that every day. My knees hurt, and I blamed it on my ski days from when I was younger. But the pain of staying the same still outweighed the pain of pushing through my runs, so I kept running.

I decided that if I was going to continue to follow through, I needed to set a goal that would scare the shit out of me. I signed up for the most difficult race I could find. It was called the Great Canadian Death Race, and it was about seven months away. The premise of the race is to run up and down three full mountain peaks in the Canadian Rockies. The distance spreads over 125 kilometers, which is almost three full marathons, but with added rocky terrain and steep mountains to climb and descend throughout. It was divided into five legs and had to be completed within twenty-four hours, or you would be disqualified. I wasn't stupid enough to go from two blocks to 125 kilometers in seven months, so I assembled a relay team with three military friends who were clearly more experienced and in better shape than I was. The understanding was that the hardest leg of the race was reserved for me. My leg would cover two of the three mountain peaks, with nearly two kilometers (sixty-three hundred feet) of elevation climb over the span of twenty-seven kilometers. For perspective, stack the Eiffel Tower in Paris, France, nearly seven times to visualize the equivalent of the climb. Much of the territory had such a steep incline on the way up that it was less of a run and more of a crawl on hands and knees. Then, of course, there was still the distance to cover. For a guy who could barely run a city block, twenty-seven kilometers was a stretch.

I signed up for an organized challenge because it kept me accountable and created an external goal with a clear finish line. A simple goal of losing weight and running a lot left too much ambiguity. If I left it at that, I could let myself off the hook at any time, and no one would really know or care. But if I was to finish a race like this, I couldn't fake it. I couldn't slack, and I couldn't lie about my goal. It was a clear one, and I had a long way to go with a short amount of time to get there. I had heard enough stories from others about increasing their distances over time, so I copied the strategy. I started by running one kilometer without a break. Then, after week one, I increased to one and a half kilometers, and a week later, I doubled it and went for three kilometers. Each run felt unnatural and painful, but I just kept thinking of melting my fat away, and at the same time, I was scared shitless of this race I had entered.

I would have these internal conversations with myself that began as a hesitation to get started. Then, as I started moving my legs, the self-talk would turn positive. I thought, *Hey, this is working well. I got this!* But a few minutes later, as I got tired, I turned back to this feeling of defeat. I kept thinking, *This is too hard. What's the point? Is it really worth it? You have lots of work to do, and you're getting behind. Doctors say running isn't good for you anyway. You don't see your family enough as it is, and you're out here punishing yourself, for what?* But I would quiet that voice down, sometimes just by drowning the noise out with good music from my headphones. I would constantly try to push myself just a little more each day. Within a few months, I was running ten kilometers, then fifteen, and by month four, on my twenty-fifth birthday, I decided to see if I could run from my house all the way to my mother's house, which was halfway across the city. I did it, and it turns out the distance was the perfect equivalent of a half marathon.

Now I was hooked. Even though it still hurt and the voices in my head continued to show up with almost every single run, I realized it was simply a game I was playing with myself—a fat devil on one shoulder and a fit angel on the other. Which version of myself would I listen to today? I started enjoying the pain that accompanied the game because I knew how good I'd feel at the end. My confidence was building. When I started my day with a good run, my workday was better because my psyche was better. I spoke to my colleagues and clients with more enthusiasm, and I felt like I could push through other life challenges with less doubt. I was also down thirty pounds, and my man-boobs disappeared, which didn't hurt.

FIND A WAY

As I pushed myself, I never researched proper running technique (or proper nutrition, for that matter). My hips began to get incredibly tight, and after a while, I started getting a shooting pain on the side of my knee. It was so bad that, multiple times, my leg would completely seize, and I would have to limp my way home from the run. I was two months away from the race, and I thought I was done for. Every day I kept trying to push through it, and the pain just wouldn't go away. It got worse, so I went to a physiotherapist, where I learned about iliotibial (IT) bands. I'd never heard of them, as I'd never studied anything related to the body, but I learned that they're long pieces of connective tissue that run from the hip to the shinbone. Mine were tightened up so hard that they were the culprit for my hip and knee pain. It was going to take a lot of work and time to loosen them up. No matter what I tried, just one run would spoil my recovery and wind my IT bands right back up.

There was no way I could continue to run and have my IT bands recover well enough to get me through that race. On the other hand, there was no way I could stop training and strictly focus on recovery. If I did nothing for two months in an attempt to recover, I wouldn't have the stamina to get through my race. It felt like a checkmate, but I wasn't ready to quit on my commitment—not after I'd announced it to my friends and colleagues along with my relay team. I couldn't live with the shame of quitting. I decided I would start swimming to keep up my endurance while I rehabbed my IT bands. But there was one problem. The only thing I was worse at than my start in running... was swimming. My wife told me I looked like a drowning seal with a missing flipper. Dammit! It felt like it took an eternity just to swim from one end of the pool to the next. I'd never tasted so much chlorine water as I did in the first week, but I was determined to get past it.

In business, my coach taught us how to achieve sustainable growth in sales. The principle was to increase your revenue by 27 percent each year. It's a digestible, achievable number that is still a stretch. If you can sustain that, your business will double every three years. That's not too daunting a goal. It's a realistic one, and if you just focus on that, you won't become paralyzed by lofty future goals that are so far away from where you currently stand. My business coach argued that we tend to overestimate what we can do in the short term, and we underestimate what we can do in the long term. If we overreach within an unrealistic amount of time, we feel discouraged when we miss our target. It feels even more out of reach, and rather than adjusting our timeline, we adjust our dreams and ultimately settle for less, in fear of another future disappointment. As a consequence, we eventually undershoot our long-term goals because the fear of failure triggers our ignorance around the power of the compounding effect.

THE COMPOUNDING EFFECT

What do I mean by "the compounding effect?" If I give you one dollar, how many times would you need to double it to reach $1 million? Is it fifty times? One hundred? Five hundred? Try doing it right now.

1, 2, 4, 8, 16, 32, 64, 128, 256, 512, 1,024, 2,048, 4,096, 8,192, 16,384, 32,768, 65,536, 131,072, 262,144, 524,288, 1,048,576.

The answer is twenty. To reach $1 million, your one dollar needs to double only twenty times. The first few multiples don't seem too exciting, but the increases gradually grow more significant. When you've doubled it nineteen times, you're still only halfway there. The very last multiple produces half of the entire result, even though the effort was the same as the very first one. This is the power of compounding. It also demonstrates the power of consistency. Doubling your goal each period is incredibly lofty in most cases, but this exercise is simply to illustrate the point. Compounding interest isn't just for finances. It works for all our efforts in life.

This principle worked incredibly well for me in business, so I decided to apply it to my swimming. I started with ten lengths, and it was absolute hell. As I learned to calm myself, I realized I was making my job harder by not synchronizing my breath with my strokes. So I worked on that. In a short(ish) amount of time, the effort required to get from one end to the next dissipated. The next time out, I tried three extra lengths, and then four extra lengths, and with almost every swim, something new clicked. By week two, I was swimming twenty-five lengths, but by the sixth week, I was swimming 120 lengths! Truly, the only reason I stopped was because I would run out of time and needed to get to work. I was feeling pretty damn good about myself each day.

As I surprised myself with my own progress, I began my swims expecting the mental challenge that was to come. I crashed consistently between lengths ten to twenty, and each time, I wondered if today just wasn't my day. I wondered if my diet was off or if my bad sleep meant it wasn't worth continuing that day. I tried to convince myself that stopping early one day might be good for me, and I could pick it back up tomorrow. But I never gave in to that little voice. I knew that if I quit once, it would be easier to quit again, so I pushed through. After getting past that wall, it would become easier again. Almost every swim beat the shit out of me as I neared my target for the day, but once I got really close, another surge of energy would come through me. If I had the time, I just kept going. It was no longer a chore to get to the pool because I looked forward to that mental battle. The pain that came with the push, and the mood that would swing from feeling defeated to this aggressive mental takeover of *playing to win*, made me feel incredible. Every. Single. Time.

THE FINISH LINE

Swimming allowed me to keep my stamina up for the Death Race while giving my IT bands a break, and it inadvertently forced me to learn a new life skill. I was ready to start running again, and over the few weeks before the race, I slowly incorporated running back into my routine, swapping between a run and a swim in an effort to prevent my IT bands from tightening before the race.

When the big day finally came, I was fifty pounds lighter, and I matched my weight from the ninth grade. The race was grueling and tough. With almost two kilometers of elevation, some of the areas were a slow crawl on all fours— mostly because my muscles were seized and my energy was depleted. It was grueling, but I looked forward to the climbs because the flats were so hard on my IT bands. Even worse, though, were the descents. With every step I took, my toes would ram the front of my shoes. About three hours in, with eight kilometers left to go, I had to stop to take my shoes off and investigate. My big toenail had peeled right off. If you've ever experienced what it feels like to have raw skin exposed beneath your toenails, you'll understand my pain. It is brutal! At the same time, my IT bands had tightened so much that I couldn't bend my hips or my knees, but I had a third of the race left to go, and I wasn't quitting. I borrowed tape from another runner and taped my toenail back on in an effort to insulate it from the friction of my socks. As I hit the road in an attempt to cross the finish line, I must've looked quite funny running stiff-legged while simultaneously trying to keep pressure off my right toe. Now all the pressure was on my left toe, and my left toenail was coming off next.

In just under four and a half hours, I hobbled across the finish line of the toughest competition I'd ever joined. I was beat up, stiff, and depleted, but I'd never felt better. I had set a goal eight months earlier, and I never let myself quit. I had a million reasons to justify why it was a bad idea, but I never gave in to those voices. I wasn't a good runner and probably not a great swimmer, but I learned something about myself over that period that no one will ever take away from me. I now understood clearly that when I make the choice to do so, I can become someone I previously wasn't—someone who can achieve something that the present or past Jeremy could never accomplish. There are no words to appropriately describe the feeling you get when you finally understand your personal power.

THE PUSH

As I built up my mental strength and stamina, I built up my self-trust, discovering that I can get through anything I want when I make a *true* decision. I don't need to have the skills or knowledge now to get it done. I just need to start. Then I need to commit. I need to follow through and push myself each day. I have to inch the wall that represents my best just a few notches forward each time I get after it. The way I get there hardly ever goes according to plan because life throws things at me that I don't expect, but those are walls I can either slam right through, jump over, or move around. Situations don't have to be linear just because they're what we imagine before we start.

This pushing forward becomes addictive and, when you continue to do it, the compounding effects of your daily efforts will eventually carry you into a new world. They will develop a part of you that you probably never knew existed. Then you'll know you can hang with those people you admired before, the ones who you thought were blessed with something special that you didn't have—and you didn't have it, but you figured out how to get it. You start to understand that your previous paradigm was bullshit. It was an excuse for you to stay small because often, the pain you imagine before you do something seems to outweigh the benefits you'll receive. Once you experience it, you realize the pain that comes from the push is precisely what makes it all feel so good. Pain hardly ever feels good in the moment, but when you keep your eye on the prize, and you don't allow it to paralyze you, then you can embrace it and, in a crazy way, you learn to love it.

This theory isn't simply for physical goals. It's for life. It's for your work. It's for family. It's for accomplishing anything in your life. The pain that comes with relationships, with new ventures, with anything that serves your values, is a necessary part of the process you must learn not to run away from, not to simply accept, but to love. You might fear it, but if there's a pain stifling your ability to live your values, if pain is precisely the thing that stands between you and your goals, the only solution is to deal with it. Run through it, over it, or around it. Do whatever it takes and don't wait, because time won't make it easier. The person you would be proud to become is waiting on the other side, and it's worth it, every fucking time.

CHAPTER 6

COURAGE AND PAIN

———

Dealing with pain is difficult. Especially new pain that we've never experienced. When faced with such pain, we often imagine the worst outcomes possible, so it hardly ever seems logical to run toward it if we have the opportunity not to deal with it at all. Escaping or ignoring it may be the best choice in some cases, but I'm not convinced it is nearly as often as we assume. In fact, the imagination of the pain before it even happens is often worse than the real thing.

Moving through pain is precisely the start of growth, and growth carries us into a new and better world. When the person you are (or, at least, the person you've been up to this point) is not equipped to deal with a circumstance, nothing on the outside can help. Instead, you are forced to go deep within yourself to find what is needed of you.

Imagine yourself as a forest. Each tree within you represents a piece of your character. One tree doesn't form the landscape, but collectively, they make up an entity. Over the vast span of its life, a forest expands and contracts, constantly becoming a different version of itself, because no individual tree in a forest has been there forever. As old ones die, new ones come to life.

Before a tree can come to be what we eventually recognize, it originates as a tiny seed buried deep below the earth's surface. With time and energy, the seed eventually sprouts. It slowly makes its way through the ground and begins its life as a sapling. As it receives nourishment from nature's elements, it eventually grows tall and strong—similar to the others around it. Our personal qualities (our character) work in the same way.

The first element required to grow is oxygen, which, in this analogy, represents life. Just as a forest requires oxygen for its trees to grow, people also need to experience life and all of its circumstances in order to mature. When we retreat in an attempt to escape from life's challenges, we're depriving ourselves of the "oxygen" necessary to develop our character.

The second element required is sun. The sun provides light, which allows us to see, and warmth, which allows us to feel. Sunlight provides to a forest the energy necessary for the trees' nourishment, enabling them to thrive in their environment. When we experience life in constant confusion, wondering why things happen the way they do, it's as if we're living in the dark. We're depriving ourselves not only of what we can see, but also of what we can feel. This is, perhaps, why we crave enlightenment. As we begin to truly understand ourselves, other people, and the natural laws in the workings of life, we can better process each circumstance. When we understand why things happen, why we feel certain emotions, and why we behave in certain ways, we become better equipped to navigate ourselves within each experience. In effect, we're enabled to constantly grow stronger and wiser. This is why nourishing our minds with good reading, good conversation, and reflective writing is incredibly important. It allows us to make sense of our experiences. Though it happens slowly, when we realize that there's no end to unfolding the mysteries of life's workings, we can finally appreciate that this is precisely the point of life: to experience its many facets, to process them, and to grow from them.

Just as the trees need sun forever to keep growing, we need to enlighten ourselves continuously. The learning never stops because when we stop growing, we start dying. With this in mind, we can let go of our attachment to getting somewhere specific in life—just to be disappointed later when we still feel like we have to keep moving. We can stop being surprised that life continues to bring us challenges years after we've battled our way through so many already.

As the cliché goes, "Life is a journey, not a destination." If you can appreciate that what you're presently dealing with is giving you exactly the lesson you need in order to grow, you'll never need to be anxious about your future.

Moving *through* pain allows us to discover who we really are and who we're capable of becoming. As we're faced with the trials of life, we develop the qualities required to get through them. If we subscribe to this outlook as a way of living, it all becomes easier to bear because we've given meaning to our suffering. We isolate one circumstance from the next and accept that, though it's not the fun part, it's precisely the circumstance we need in order to become who we're meant to be (and only if we allow it). The more we're tested, the more seeds fall to the ground, gifting us the opportunity to develop more of our character. As this process continues, the growth takes on a life of its own, and we become strengthened not by one "tree" or by five, but by thousands. We would hardly be recognized by anyone who hadn't been there to see the process from the beginning. This doesn't happen over days or months. For a forest, it happens over decades and centuries. For us, it happens over years and decades, and it continues as long as we allow it to.

CHOICE

There's a third element necessary to all that growth. Just

as a tree cannot grow solely with sun and oxygen, humans cannot grow simply by experiencing life and understanding it. Trees also need water, and they require a proactive practice to get it. For what we see of a tree above the ground, there's a much more intricate component below that is hidden from plain sight. A tree's roots grow deep below the ground in search of water. From our viewpoint, we see direct, linear growth—a tall, straight trunk with branches coming off all sides. Externally, it looks quite simple, but below the surface, the tree's root system is complex. It grows beneath the earth with veins constantly spreading in each direction, sometimes weaving over and around the veins of other trees, grounding itself, and strengthening its ability to stand in place, all in the process of the search for water. The process strengthens not only the one tree, but also those around it. As we look back above the surface, we see that the more a tree spreads its roots, the harder it becomes for life's elements to knock it down. The tree's strength doesn't simply come from its big trunk above the ground, but from the mighty roots below. Hence the term *grounded*.

Humans have an added element of challenge: the ability to consciously choose. From a metaphysical standpoint, we can choose to grow, or we can choose not to. If we choose growth, we need to conquer the fear that holds us back from doing so. *Our* roots are our values, and the water we seek that helps us to grow is courage. With conscious intention, our roots grow deeper within, searching for the courage required to live our values. The roots of each value intertwine and fortify as we become grounded in our personal choices. Externally, the elements of life that challenge us have a harder time knocking us down.

In our attempts to succeed in the real world, we tend to focus on external strength over internal. We focus on what we and others can see. Though it can work to some degree, when life's elements really test us, weak roots simply won't be able to hold us up. This is why we must practice courage in living our values, not simply in the big things, but in the small ones and in those that others cannot see.

Courage is not the absence of fear but the ability to act in spite of it. Fear exists in all of us. It serves a necessary function in our ability to survive. If our ancestors hadn't been scared of the saber-toothed tiger, they wouldn't have run or fought from an attack, and our race would no longer exist. Simply put, fear is the awareness of our vulnerability. It is a function of our ego—the awareness of the *self*. If we're not aware of our vulnerability, we eventually get burned. Fear prompts a reaction of self-preservation. Bearing this in mind, it doesn't have only one strategy in its arsenal. Fear can trigger us to run away, it can trigger anger, and it can trigger paralysis. (We "smart ones" often disguise *paralysis* as *analysis*.) But fear can also trigger action—specifically, combative action. Each one of those responses serves its purpose in different situations. We often forget to question which reaction would serve us best within a given situation, but each response is learned and, therefore, can be unlearned if we feel it necessary to our growth. Reactions are muscles that we build, and when intention and effort are absent, we default to the one we use most often, with little regard to the outcome it tends to draw.

Courage is our ability to deal with fear and to choose which response serves us best, regardless of our initial inclination. The less we practice it, the less natural it will feel, because it requires inner combat. We have to fight the more natural responses of flight, inaction, or anger—none of which requires courage. Those reactions are often present, and they trick our subconscious into moving toward preservation. The trick works because it's not a lie. Self-preservation is precisely what those reactions accomplish. They keep us from summoning that new part of us that needs to develop so we become better equipped to deal with the world of tomorrow. Humans are meant for growth. Just like the trees from a forest, if we aren't growing, we are dying. As it turns out, self-preservation is a lie.

CONTAGION OF ENERGY

When trees combine water and sunlight, they create their own oxygen. Scientists know this as photosynthesis. It is the reason trees are so important to life on this earth. But how did it all start? The tree needs oxygen from the environment to begin its growth; then later, it contributes to producing the oxygen that we and all other life requires. It is the cycle of life that keeps it all going. When humans practice courage and learn about ourselves and about life, our growth also creates new energy. It sparks the idea of new possibilities for ourselves and for others. As we begin to realize what we're capable of, we produce a newfound excitement for life. We are the benefactors, but so are the others around us because energy is contagious. Like the tree that creates oxygen for itself, the forest, and the rest of the world, we do the same for ourselves, our peers, and eventually for the rest of the world. It's easy to dismiss that and call bullshit, but just like oxygen from trees, the energy we create is still there—despite the fact that we can't see, hear, smell, taste, or touch it. That is the power we each must learn to live with.

When we don't produce enough of our own energy, we depend on the energy that others create. That is why negative people leave us feeling tired. They are literally sucking the energy out of us. Because they aren't producing enough of their own, they need some of ours to survive. Conversely, we feel so alive after meeting someone who inspires us because they are producing more energy than they can consume. We not only receive their energy, but with it we create more as we build on the thought or activity they shared. We know this as *momentum*, but we typically don't ponder how it works or where it comes from. Think of Martin Luther King Jr.'s "I have a dream" speech. We can watch or simply read the speech, nearly sixty years after it was first delivered, and still be moved, not just by King's passion, but by his ideal that speaks to something most of us probably know as truth. His thoughts and emotions produced an energy that still lives, long past his death.

If you're a hockey fan, think of game seven of the playoff finals. The energy in that arena and in our living rooms as we watch is not the same as a regular-season game. It's electrifying, and you don't need to understand hockey to feel it. It's the same sport with the same rules and players as any other game in the season. But it's completely different, simply because of the narrative. The stakes are higher, and the stars set the tone for the way the game is played. The intensity of every play is cranked up. The fans, coaches, and players all know they have something big to win or lose, and it all depends on this one game, right now.

But that is all a story we accept as a group. Someone decided that the final game was the one that made all the difference. They decided that the ultimate prize to covet is a hunk of metal shaped like the cereal bowl in your kitchen cupboard. It is the thing that tens of thousands of people devote their entire lives to obtaining. Since enough of us subscribe to that story, it works. Of course, this doesn't just apply to hockey. Sports are a perfect example of how we create energy and build momentum in life, of how energy is contagious, and we don't even need to participate in the activity to benefit from it. Otherwise, sports would have only players and no fans. The energy is so contagious that teams can create superfans who devote their lives to watching an activity that they don't even play themselves—some so religiously that their psychological well-being depends on the fates of their teams. If you're a Seahawks fan and the Seahawks lose, it's a terrible day, and you have much to blame for the injustices of the world. If you're a Lakers fan and they win, all is right in the world. It's easy to hide behind sports teams because we share in the glories of their successes on the court or the field, but we don't need to work ourselves through the years of pain, the disappointments, and the hard work that the athletes sacrificed to get there. We might admire that part of the sport, but we certainly don't need to participate in it. Yet when the lights are on and it's game time, the energy the athletes create is shared with us. If you've ever wondered why a middle-class family will spend a week's salary to attend just one game, now you know.

We rely so much on our five senses that we think only of food as our source of energy (yet, ironically, we can't get that right either). Mental and spiritual energy are equally important to our survival and growth, and they work together. One feeds the other and, just as good energy builds momentum, so does bad energy. Unhealthy foods offer a short spike in energy and later make us feel tired, just as unhealthy thoughts do. They build momentum, making it harder for us to escape. When we engage in complaining, bickering, and victimization, we feed off that energy, and our minds go to work to prove our thoughts right, so we look for more reasons that something isn't working or that someone is doing something they shouldn't. For this reason, be mindful of the information you take in each day. Be mindful of the conversations your friends and coworkers have or the posts on your Facebook feed. The seeds of each thought grow and eventually crowd your headspace. It would serve you well to make sure it's information that serves you.

CHAPTER 7

COURAGE LEADS TO CONFIDENCE

——

When I started my career in real estate, I told myself that I was shy. That was the story I'd told myself since I was four years old; therefore, every interaction I had with others was a fight with my own natural tendency toward shyness. I knew that if I was to succeed in sales, I couldn't be shy—at least not when I was working. When I put my shirt and tie on in the morning before an appointment, I would tell myself a different story. I told myself that I was successful, confident, and outgoing. I envisioned what I wanted my clients to see in me, and I used inspiration from agents I'd met who exuded those qualities. It was almost as if I created an alter ego. I've never been one to pretend I am anything I'm not, so this was a challenge for me. It turned out that the more I put myself out there, the better I projected this new side of myself—an outgoing side that eventually made me feel more comfortable in my own skin. Depending how I feel on certain days, I still need to have that active self-talk before meeting a client, speaking in public, or playing music in front of others. I need to tell myself that I am comfortable with myself, and then my behavior falls in line to prove me right. With each experience, my confidence grows.

When you take a thought and hold it in your mind, you are consciously or subconsciously allowing it to grow. As you act it out and share it, it takes on a life of its own. We look for ways to prove ourselves right, and we act in accordance with that thought. Therefore, to become someone we have never been, we must tell ourselves that we are already that person. As we tell ourselves a different story, we look for ways to turn it into reality. The more we act in spite of our fears, the more we nourish the seed of a new character trait. It doesn't often happen overnight, but as we continue to challenge ourselves, we eventually look back and realize that we accomplished what we set out to become.

THE SEED

Acts of courage don't need to be massive feats. We all love to hear stories of people doing amazing things that seem almost surreal. They might inspire us in the moment, but if we haven't built up our muscles of courage in the small acts, it's even more difficult to attempt the big ones. When we fail, we become discouraged and take on the belief that we don't have what it takes. If I've never physically worked out before, I can't walk into a gym and bench press two hundred pounds. It's a terrible idea, and I will fail. I'm better served to start simply with the bar, then add a few pounds. After a few weeks, I can add a few more as I grow comfortable with the movement and the weight. It doesn't look sexy to lift a bar with a few puny weights on it, but as I learn to enjoy the process, I can celebrate the small wins that come only with time. Eventually, as my muscles strengthen, two hundred pounds will seem light to me. Then, when I trace my steps back to consider my progress, I'll realize that I'm now doing the very thing that inspired me to start. As it turns out, I had what it took all along. I just needed to *develop* it.

Confidence is a process. It requires patient, consistent effort, and it always starts simply with a seed. Sometimes results come slowly, and sometimes they come fast. Be careful not to set expectations based on what you see of others. It might rob you of the very confidence you're working to build. But you must start, and you must train your mind to believe it's possible. Whatever you believe, your mind will go to work to prove you right, and your actions will follow your thoughts. It will become a self-fulfilling prophecy. This is why a negative mind can take your life in a completely different direction than a positive one. If you love to consume information that lives in the negative, you develop a habit of living inside of problems rather than living in solutions. We're physically on the same planet, but we end up living in entirely different worlds based on the polarity of our minds. When we believe that everything is happening *to us* rather than *for us*, we're refusing to accept our own personal power. We deny ourselves the opportunities not only to build a better life externally, but to build a stronger mind. We need a stronger mind because, with a weak one, we cannot build true confidence.

JUST WAIT

You might contest that there are several things in life that we can't control, and I would agree—it's delusional to think otherwise. I can't control the weather. I can't control the pandemic that's consuming our world as I write this. I can't control the economy. I couldn't control my father's drug addictions. I can't control the behavior of the people in my life. But I can always control how I respond to them. The conversations I have with myself through any situation will determine my perception, and that will determine how I handle it. Circumstances out of my control might put a wrench in the spokes, spoiling my plans for how I believed the future would look, or at least how I might get there. But they might not. If I remind myself that life is happening *for me* rather than *to me*, I can be grateful in spite of the suffering I might endure. I can look for meaning in any event, no matter how harsh it is in the moment. If it's a painful experience, I can remind myself that all things pass, as long as I allow them to. That thought doesn't necessarily relieve me of the pain in that moment, but it reminds me that it won't be there forever.

When we feel intense emotion from an occurrence, we tend to live in that emotion as if it's permanent—like our entire world has been shaken up, past, present, and future. But if we train ourselves to step back—right now, inside the moment—we remind ourselves that just as we can count on the seasons of fall, winter, spring, and summer to arrive each year, we can count on our circumstances to continuously change. When things are bad, just wait. And when things are good, just wait. But in the waiting, we should be cautious not to curse the season of our circumstance. It's a part of life that will continue to come, and therefore it would serve us well to accept it, to look for its lesson, and maybe even to eventually appreciate it.

You can accept that, though an event may bring permanent change, unless it's a true life-or-death situation, *you* will arrive intact in the future regardless. With that, you can bring wonder to what comes next, rather than worry. The future hasn't happened yet, so anything you ponder is simply your imagination, which you have full control of. You can imagine possibilities that excite you, or you can imagine possibilities that you dread. Whichever you choose, you should remember that your mind will go to work to prove you right, and your actions will follow. With this in mind, it would serve you well to question whether you're making the best use of your imagination.

JUST DO IT

It's difficult to summon courage when we don't believe in the possibility of what that courageous act might bring. If we're focused on the worst possible outcome, how likely are we to take the required steps? Life is easier to bear when we're pulled by excitement rather than pushed by fear, but either one is better than being paralyzed by the notion that our life's circumstances are of no consequence to our own behavior. If this were true, there would be no point to life. There would be no one doing amazing things that inspire us. No Nelson Mandela, no Michael Jordan, no Mother Teresa, Albert Einstein, or Martin Luther King Jr. Our actions, led by our beliefs—good or bad—make a difference not only to ourselves but also to the ones around us.

If that feels like too big of a responsibility, we might choose *inaction* as a safe bet. *Let's let life determine what's next so we don't fuck it up and accidentally make it worse.* But inaction itself is also a choice we make, and it's often a subconscious one guided by a fear we hold—one that we don't want to accept. Inaction allows us to fly under the radar and hide our true selves from ourselves. Every single living being on this planet serves a purpose, and humans might carry the largest responsibility. Why? We are the ones most capable of consciously choosing our thoughts and behavior, and with that, we affect the direction of our lives and of those involved, no matter what we do—or don't do. Taking action in accordance with our authentic needs and desires requires courage because those needs and desires are vulnerable. Our nature is to protect vulnerable things and, therefore, we often envelop them with fear. Courage is the vehicle that moves us through our fear and allows us to connect with our authentic selves. It allows us to achieve what we're really after.

Maybe you're thinking, *But what if I don't know what I actually want?* I believe we always know what we want, deep down. The problem is that we often can't articulate it, but that doesn't mean it's not there. If we feel like something is missing inside, then a desire surely exists. We just haven't developed it yet, and it's possible that we're trying too hard to figure it out. When we try too hard, we can't relax. We become rigid in our thinking and attach ourselves to what we think we might be looking for. Then confusion sets in when we don't see it. Don't try too hard. Instead, focus on the small things in life that you already know need to change. Make small acts of courage that compound in strength, and over time, the fog will dissipate and your vision will become clearer.

CHAPTER 8

JUMP—A COURAGE CASE STUDY

———

I couldn't stop watching YouTube videos of people doing parkour. Parkour was first developed by the French military as a way to quickly and efficiently get up and over objects. Also known as freerunning, it completely defies what we thought the human body was capable of doing. The athletes use their own bodies' momentum to jump over objects and to roll out the absorption of the impact from falls. They use their hands and feet almost as four-legged animals do. They jump from wall end to wall end, switching directions by pushing off with one leg and carrying the momentum to drive themselves up and over walls that humans shouldn't be capable of climbing. It looks like all the stunts in the James Bond movies that we just thought were fake but entertaining to watch. Watching those scenes, most of us would think, *Wouldn't it be cool if we could move like superheroes?* Well, it turns out those movements are real, and they can be learned.

I was so infatuated with parkour that I wanted to learn it myself. The old me would have let that desire sit until the feeling passed by. I was already working crazy hours, and I had kids, a wife, two dogs, and my workouts to manage. Besides, I was already in my thirties, and parkour is certainly a young person's sport. The old me would've said I should just continue watching the videos and dreaming that it's me doing those things. Sometimes, fantasizing about these things inside my head can be pretty satisfying. I can pretend that it's me doing all the stunts right from my couch, and then, when I'm done, I can just get up and get back to what I'm doing. I don't have to go through the pain of trying and sucking. There's no getting hurt and no time taken away from the million things I already have going on.

Fantasizing about being better at things than we actually are can be really satisfying, but we're not meant to leave it at that. The fantasy is meant to inspire us to figure out how to make it a reality. The former is the equivalent of obsessing over a sports team. It's not the same glory as actually playing. It's not the same satisfaction, and it doesn't truly make us come alive. It's good entertainment and serves a purpose, but I've learned that doing is much more satisfying that watching. I was ready to be a participant and not just a spectator. But where to start?

I researched parkour classes and, because it's a relatively

new sport, I found that there was one single company offering classes in my city, and they were mostly for kids, not grown adults with no gymnastics background and questionable coordination. Digging a little farther, I saw that they offered one adult class. I thought, *This is perfect!* But then, when I got to registration, I saw that adults were classified as ages sixteen and older. I started thinking more about it and realized they probably did that because there aren't enough adults my age who would take a class like this. I imagined showing up alone with no one I knew, and participating with a bunch of boys young enough to be my kids. Then I thought, *I'm not very well coordinated. I don't even attempt to dance because I have two left feet. I'm going to look ridiculous in front of these kids. What was I thinking? It was just another stupid fantasy.*

LEARNING TO DREAM

If you're accustomed to putting yourself out there and trying new things, this might not seem like a big deal to you. But I had homeschooled when I was younger and then essentially became an adult at fourteen, never trying anything new other than job changes, which were less voluntary than an obligation to survive. Those changes were necessities, and therefore there was no reason to debate whether I should or shouldn't do something. This was the first time no person or circumstance was prodding me to do something. I was doing it without accountability to anyone else, and if I'd decided not to, no one would ever know but me. My life wouldn't be affected in the least if I didn't go—or at least, that's how I rationalized it. So I opted out of registering and forced myself to forget all about it. But those damn videos kept popping up on my social media feeds.

Part of my business coaching had trained me on how to dream. My coach suggested that early in the morning, before we start our workday, we should prime our minds and get excited about our future. One of the exercises he suggested we use for this is called Future Focus. The exercise is to take each of the seven areas of our lives (family, intimate, financial, physical, spiritual, mental, and professional) and write a paragraph for each, describing *not* how things are, but how we would like them to be in five years' time. We're not to focus on how we would achieve it, but simply what the perfect reality would look like. Thinking about the *how* blocks our creativity and influences what we write. The focus is to dream without inhibition.

I found this practice incredibly inspiring, and I already trusted the process. I knew that it worked because, the year before, I had reread what I had written the very first time, five years prior. I felt chills run through my entire body as I read through an almost perfect description of my current life. I had written about the community I lived in, what my house looked like, what my family looked like, my business, my revenue, my net worth, my relationship, and even the car I was driving. At least 80 percent of it had come true, and this was no accident. Writing it out gave me a direction, an aim, something that inspired me. It's not a document that I read every day, but more a "set it and forget it" dream planner. Even without reviewing it daily, writing my dreams in vivid detail ingrained them into my subconscious and guided me to make decisions that aligned with those dreams. Don't ask me to explain the science behind it any more than that. All I know is it worked, and if nothing else, it was a fun exercise.

My business coach also encouraged us to write out a Dream List. We wrote down fifty things we would like to see, experience, or accomplish before we die—another great exercise to clarify our desires and get us excited. The key to both of these is not to attach ourselves to them, but simply to dream. Attachment pulls us farther away from the dream because it registers in our subconscious that we *don't* have it. The Dream List causes our minds to think in possibilities, and when opportunity arises, we might make choices that better align with those dreams. If the things you write down mean something to you, it's telling you that those are things worth living for. As long as you're not hurting anyone else in their pursuit, the sacrifices are worth making. It was clear to me that I should put parkour in both my Future Focus and Dream List. I didn't concern myself with why because knowing I wanted to do it was enough.

STEPPING IN

A few months later, I finally signed up for parkour classes. I was nervous as hell, imagining myself breaking an arm or wrist or rolling my ankle. I imagined a group full of sixteen-year-old superathletes who were all buddies in a clique, talking and laughing at the old guy who sucks and doesn't belong there. But I showed up anyway. On the day of my first class, I stretched and breathed deeply and nervously, and with a brave face, I kissed my kids and my wife goodbye as if it might be the last time I would see them again. (Thank god they had no clue how terrified I was.)

Learning from my sales calls, I primed myself before arriving, and I walked in confidently. As I drove to the gym (and probably the whole day leading up to it), I visualized and imagined being my best, confident self. I thought of scenarios that might make me uncomfortable and how I would deal with that. I walked in prepared. The trainers had subleased a section of a traditional gymnastics studio. Because it was located in the back corner of the building, I had to walk past two spectator rooms, each separated by a Plexiglas wall. I walked across the first room, cutting off the view of parents my age who were watching their little girls in leotards as they performed their gymnastic routines. All their eyes redirected toward me as I distracted them from their children. I'd hoped I could blend in and pretend I was just a parent spectator too, but it was obvious I would be joining the kids, as I was walking with my gym bag with no kid beside me. I walked past the next room, and this one was reserved for the parents of the parkour kids—the ones I was about to join. Doubt set in again, and I felt out of place and exposed. I thought, *What the hell. I committed to it, so just keep moving.*

There were about twenty-five people in the class and, as I had guessed, the majority were probably between ages sixteen and twenty, but I was relieved to see there were also a few older adults. One dad was in the class with his son. Another was at least ten years older than me. There were almost as many women as men, and the people came in all shapes and sizes. As the class started, the coaches made us run in formation to warm up. We ran in a pretty tight circle, which felt awkward, and then they made us switch directions, run backward and sideways, and a few other awkward movements. It lasted a few minutes, then they guided us through some stretching. Once we finished, we all had to form a straight line, called the baseline. The coach made us introduce ourselves, stating our name and why we joined the class. As nervous as I was while waiting for my turn, I noticed that most people there, at least the new ones who had never taken the class, were just as nervous as I was. This gave me comfort. I still choked on my words when the time came for me to introduce myself, but I felt more comfortable with the company I was keeping.

The first move they taught was basic, as I expected. It was called the parkour roll. They explained that before you learn how to jump or trick, you need to learn how to fall. The move is used more often than any other. We learned to roll momentum out of our movement rather than bringing ourselves to a dead stop. Each step was thoroughly explained, and then we were given open floor time to work on the move. Each class member progressed at different levels, and the more advanced students were given bigger challenges. I felt stupid and unnatural for my first few attempts and, if I'm being honest, a little scared to even try. But as everyone continued to work on their parkour roll, so did I. It took only a few minutes before I was hooked. It was fun. Every move was taught the same way. The coaches would show us what the end result should look like, then they'd break it down and even give progression moves to build up our awareness of body mechanics. Then we'd practice the move, and with each attempt, things would come together a little more.

Flash forward a few years, and I'm still going to the gym every week. Parkour has become a staple in my life. No matter how busy or stressed I am, I let go of it all when I'm training. For that one hour each Wednesday night, I'm completely wrapped up in that single activity, and nothing else in the world matters. I don't think of my finances. I don't think of work issues. I leave my phone in my car, and I just jump around and play like I'm a kid again. When I come out of that class, not only am I full of energy, but my confidence is up, and I'm ready to tackle life.

There have been more unexpected benefits. As I continued to go to classes, I got to know the owner of the gym. We became good friends, and he's a constant in my life, as I see him on a weekly basis. 2J (yes, that's his name) continues to push me out of my comfort zone. He teaches verbally and also leads by example, showing how to take steps to slowly build confidence when applying something new. We continuously push ourselves forward, just slightly out of our comfort zones, but we don't outpace our confidence with our skill level. 2J taught me to push myself one step at a time, and not five. He showed me how to build my skills, test the waters, and never stop moving forward.

UNINTENTIONAL SKILLS

That way of life should carry into everything we do, and it shouldn't stop there. When we concern ourselves with what those around us—the spectators—think of us, we block out our own creativity. We distract ourselves from envisioning everything working out, and rather, imagine the worst possible cases. My subconscious acts out what I see in my mind in order to prove me right. I'm literally robbing myself of success by thinking of anything except what I actually want. If I can't help it, and I think about what others are thinking of me, I should make the best use of my imagination and expect them to delight in what I'm about to do. It would serve me better to do so, but it's very difficult if I've built a habit of thinking in worst-case scenarios. The only way I can accomplish this is to be unattached to that result, to release my fear that things won't go my way, and to be prepared to laugh at myself if it doesn't work out. In other words, I need to stop taking everything so damn seriously!

This unexpected skill should serve me in other areas of my life. It might serve me for writing. It might serve me for my business. It might serve me to speak in public without having an out-of-body experience and completely freezing my train of thought. It might teach me to play guitar and sing as well in front of my friends as I do when I'm locked in my room by myself. Hell, it might teach me how to learn to play and speak and write even better because I now have a framework for how to learn. I might be doing my staff and my kids a favor, because now I can teach them that framework. Or at least I can adapt it to my coaching style and better prepare them to learn what I have to teach.

My initial intention in signing up for parkour was to practice enough courage to try something uncomfortable, simply because I wanted to have fun. But the benefits went way beyond what I expected. I became fitter and more coordinated, and I built another block of confidence. I learned not to take myself so seriously and to play without inhibitions, as we do so naturally when we're children. I gained friends who taught me what I needed most—perhaps what was responsible for my ability to write this book. I got out of my head and unattached myself from the fear of being judged. I learned to deal with the constant and irrational concern that others were watching me and drawing conclusions about my worth and credibility based strictly on what they saw in that moment. I no longer tried to control the image of what I wanted others to think. Liberating myself from that way of living for over thirty years was the start of a freedom for which words can't do justice.

This is not an instant cure. It was, and still is, a work in progress, but nonetheless, the seed sprouted and began to develop. The story isn't about parkour. It's about the small act of moving myself toward something I was drawn to. I wasn't looking for any benefit aside from doing something that looked cool on YouTube. Yes, small acts of courage establish your sense of power, but you never know how you and others in your life will truly benefit from taking action in spite of your fear—even when you think that action is inconsequential. Trying something new may or may not transform you into a new person, but consistent acts of courage will.

CHAPTER 9

COURAGE AND RELATIONSHIPS

———

In my first few years living with my girlfriend and now wife, Avarey and I would fight about the stupidest things. Our most notable fight was when she decorated the guest bathroom in hot pink. As you can imagine, nothing said was mature or rational on either end. Somehow that stupid bathroom brought out the worst in us, and this microscopic life detail tested our ability to agree on anything bigger in life.

Sometimes, getting through fights with loved ones—even over simple things like paint colors—requires small but incredibly difficult feats of courage. These fights can touch on all sorts of underlying issues, and before we know it, we're no longer arguing about the issue that originally sparked the conflict but, instead, about all the things we'd previously held ourselves back from resolving.

Every one of us lives a different life, but because we all hold individual fears and insecurities, it's up to us to individually reflect on where we might want to inject courage. There are common fears we all face, and among them are relationships with other people. Though we may experience relationships differently, dynamics with other humans can be incredibly difficult. Whether it's with our friends, coworkers, spouse, or family members, we're guaranteed to be faced with challenges that we won't want to face. We're eventually (and often) faced with conflict from bad communication, poor treatment, unfair judgment, misaligned values, or a plethora of other causes. How we deal with these conflicts makes all the difference in determining the end result.

You get what you tolerate—from people, from yourself, and from life. What are you accepting, brushing off, or rationalizing as good intentions that you could do without? It's never easy to have these discussions, but the most difficult conversations are the most important ones to have. Conflict is something most of us like to avoid (unless you prefer to live in constant conflict, in which case you may want to consider finding a way to make peace with yourself). Conflict can make situations worse if it isn't properly handled. Rather than taking the risk of mishandling things, we often let them go. The problem with that strategy is that we've usually tricked ourselves into believing that we actually let it go, when the truth is that we buried it. Burying a feeling doesn't kill it. It allows the emotion to fester and grow as it lies dormant, hidden from our conscious mind. Eventually, when we least expect it, a spark—often a simple act similar to the one that initially bugged us—will ignite and blow the buried emotion out of us, surprising not only the other person involved, but also ourselves. This is when we lose control of our rationality and we do or say something damaging. Once we finally calm down, we think, *Where the fuck did that come from?*

If someone is bothering us, and we know that bringing it up in conversation will turn into a fight that's likely not productive, we instead have the conversation in our own mind. We build hypothetical responses, making assumptions on how that conversation would go and even on how the other person thinks and feels. Because we think we're smarter than most people and we can read them by their body language, we assume we don't need to talk it through. We think, *I already know.* With that mindset, we might conclude that the relationship just isn't worth having. Maybe the other person isn't meant to be in our lives. Maybe it was a good thing up until now, but we've grown apart, and life would just be better if we went our separate ways. With that, we might give up and start fresh. So we move on to a new friendship or romantic relationship, a new job, or a new team. Maybe it goes really well for some time, but eventually we're faced with the same issues. Maybe not the exact same, but nonetheless, we're faced yet again with uncomfortable circumstances. We wonder why this keeps happening to us.

It happens because it's a part of life. All humans view life through their own lens. No matter how aligned two people are, we have our own life circumstances, our own needs and desires, and our own issues that influence our moods. We each filter how we see a circumstance through the experiences of our past and the influence of others in our environment. Sometimes there's a crossover, and we catch each other at the wrong time. Even the very best relationships still encounter conflict for this reason. The difference is that those individuals don't grow apart from it, but instead, they grow stronger. They find ways to handle and resolve it, but someone has to start.

CONFLICT WITHOUT CONVERSATION

If talking through an issue will likely lead to a worse outcome, there are more options than verbal conversation. When I was just getting into my teens, my mother and I used to fight—*a lot!* We were both stubborn and couldn't articulate ourselves well. As much as she tried, her authority didn't work on me, and neither of us would allow a proper, flowing conversation. Our fights would lead to her assigning long consequences, like no friends or television for a week, but I wouldn't accept it. With conviction, I promised that I would defy her consequences if

I didn't agree with them, and there was nothing she could do about it. She followed through on her end, and so did I. My rebellion led to extensions of punishments, and I continued to do what I wanted. We were stuck with each other (not for long, as I mentioned before), and it was a tense environment.

On occasion, when things got bad, we would write each other letters. It allowed us to get everything off our chests, uninterrupted. I could explain my feelings from my point of view, and I could take all the time I needed to make sure I was properly expressing myself. Then, once she read it, she could absorb my viewpoint before she responded to explain hers. Her response would always be more sensitive to understanding how I was feeling about the situation. We didn't always agree with each other afterward, but it was always more amicable, and we found new respect for each other every time.

When Avarey and I fought about that stupid hot pink bathroom, I decided to write a letter and explain my position. I started it with the intention of proving why I was right and she was wrong. But once I read through my first draft, I saw that I sounded like a pompous jerk. No wonder she had gotten angry and verbally attacked me! The only way the letter would be effective was to first prove that I understood her position. I couldn't simply say, "I know how you feel." I needed to elaborate, and I also needed to write out the words, "I know that it's important to you," because I couldn't assume that she knew I was aware. Looking back, my body language and everything I said suggested the opposite.

I wrote to make sure my case was effective, but the simple act of writing defused my frustration and allowed me to let my guard down. I actually started to place myself in her shoes because I allowed myself the space to do so. Once she read the letter, her guard was let down as well, and she responded similarly. This act allowed us to get past our heated emotions and move on to more rational discussions in search of a win-win situation. As we worked through our issues, we became aware that it was important for Avarey to express her femininity and for me to express my adulthood (yes, I'm aware of the irony of my immaturity). This was an opportunity to learn more about each other and about ourselves. In this process of discovery, we realized that we don't need bathroom colors as an outlet. Suddenly, the pink bathroom mattered less to each of us, and the next day, it was gone.

As life progressed, we faced more issues, and each time we did, the more intense the conflict, the stronger our bond became. In the moment, however short or long, it felt like it was going the complete opposite way, tearing us apart. But when one of us mustered the courage to be vulnerable and express how we felt and what we wanted to resolve, we found common ground, and our bond grew as a result. This act was a gesture that suggested to the other that our relationship was more important than the issue, and sometimes that was all we needed for permission to work together in figuring it out. If we hadn't learned to deal with the small things, we wouldn't be as well equipped to deal with the bigger ones. Either one of us could have conceded to "let it go" without making sure we both fully understood how we felt, but that could have been one more block of resentment buried within one of us. Resentments can build upon each other and eventually lead to a blowout. Through the complex web of small, unsolved issues, we may never understand where the frustration of the blowout even came from.

It is for this reason that I'm blunt. It's a blessing and a curse, but you don't ever have to wonder if my thoughts are any different from what I project. It works well for me because I carry no resentment toward anyone (not for long, anyway). But it also hurts my relationships if I'm not careful because I might say something to someone who doesn't share that same life philosophy.

RELATIONSHIPS ARE AN INVESTMENT

Romantic relationships aren't the only ones we have. In many cases, they might be the most difficult, but that is simply because the more we integrate our life with another's, the more we have invested. The more we're invested, the higher the stakes, and the higher the stakes, the higher the emotion. The higher the emotions, the more challenging it becomes to resolve a problem. Investing in another person emotionally, financially, and socially can become incredibly complex. Therefore, when we go about our lives and neglect to communicate our thoughts, objectives, and feelings, we're defaulting to assuming that we understand each other. This allows a small seed of misalignment to silently grow completely out of our consciousness until a spark ignites and it turns to a battle.

The more we focus solely on our own needs, the bigger the challenge becomes to maintain and build a healthy relationship. Whether with a spouse, a friend, a family member, a business partner, or a client, issues will arise. When emotions run high, logical care and reason are often absent. Relationships are incredibly important, and when we learn to handle them with proper care, they become the source of all our successes in life. For this reason, it's important not to quit on them. The challenges they bring are a gift. They offer us an opportunity to grow—first ourselves and then the relationship as a consequence.

If we haven't mastered our behavior when emotions are high, the best strategy can often be to step back and create a safe space alone, to gather our thoughts to take the twenty-thousand-foot view and assess the situation through the other's eyes and mind, and to calibrate our goals so we're in alignment. For me, writing letters works incredibly well. They are responsible for saving my marriage. They are responsible for saving some of my most important friendships, and they are responsible for saving my business.

IN THE EYE OF THE STORM

The letters I write hardly ever start out as diplomatic as they are in the final draft. They start as a therapeutic outlet for me to tell the other person why I'm right and they are wrong. It feels great to write that, but I give myself time to review before I send them to the recipient. As I read the first draft, I usually realize what a pompous asshole I can be. I realize that I dismiss feelings that aren't mine, not always immediately, but over time when *I* deem that it's time for the other to get over it.

In light of this, I'm compelled to rewrite what I actually want to say. It has to start with what I love and admire about them. It has to talk about what I ultimately want — to realign our goals and our vision for what we're trying to accomplish. Life becomes cloudy when we're inside a storm of emotions. Sometimes we're consumed with survival in that moment, so we run in any direction and forget where we actually intend to go. The beautiful thing about emotional storms, as opposed to nature's, is that we can give ourselves the time to slow down and recalibrate. We have time to write out our thoughts, then read them and clarify ourselves to ourselves. Often, when we do this and reflect, we realize that our survival tool (our ego) plays tricks on us. Our inner narrative is telling the wrong story, and that's how things get out of hand. When we end up in a different direction, we don't blame ourselves for not using our inner compass. No, we blame the wind for blowing in the wrong direction. We blame the people with us for fucking up our plans with their own emotions. It's hardly ever our fault, because that's a much easier narrative to live with than the one that might steer us back in the right direction.

Steering yourself in the right direction requires reflection. It requires letting out all your thoughts and emotions without inhibition, then taking all that in as if you're someone else. We know this intuitively, and this is why we tend to "give others a piece of our minds." We share all the little things that bother us, and this is how we fight. It's important to get it out, but the problem with doing it in real time is that our emotions trigger the other's emotions, causing backlash, and that, in turn, drives our emotions up, and then our egos are in a full-out battle. The result of this lazy strategy is that we hardly ever end up where we intend. If you're a parent, you see your children in this predicament all too often. They have a hard time articulating themselves, and their arguments turn out to be an irrational battle of words where one person might become so frustrated that he gives up on using his words and resorts to expressing his pain physically. We, as adults, are only slightly more sophisticated in that our vocabulary might be larger, but our egos still respond the same way. If we're "civilized" enough not to spark an altercation, we just keep the frustration inside and allow our inner narrative to build up the frustrations even further. We think it's the diplomatic strategy to keep it inside, and we might pride ourselves on our maturity not to "stick it to someone" even though they deserve it. But the end result is the same, and often worse.

If our intention is to bring order to the chaos of our situation, we're much better served to step back and act out the frustration alone. Use that person as an imaginary recipient, either of a written letter or of a voice memo recorded on your phone. Don't hold back. Stick it to them, then play the voice memo to yourself and pretend you're the recipient. It's a wonderful way to self-reflect. Ask yourself what you're really trying to accomplish and come back to your original intention—what you *ultimately* want to accomplish.

FOCUS ON THE RIGHT PROBLEM

My mentor, Richard, often reminds me that it's very difficult to be right and happy at the same time. When we focus on being right, we're trying to solve the wrong problem. We're focused on immediate gratification rather than a long-term solution. It feels good to be right, but it hardly ever solves the problem. With that knowledge, battling our ego's need to do this is a losing strategy. We can't suppress it, and we can't ignore it because it won't die that way. We need to let it out in a safe environment where no one gets hurt. Once we let it out, we can regain awareness of our *actual* intentions—not to be right, but to accomplish what we meant to before we were sidelined. It's much like recalibrating your compass to remember which way north is. A compass has a needle that is aligned with the earth's magnetic field. We mark one end in red so as to recognize which direction is north. But that needle is delicate and can lose calibration if it's in close contact with another magnet. This is what happens to us in conflict. We lose our sense of where we're headed, and we follow our broken compass without thought. We're better served to separate our compass from the other magnet and reset it, realigning ourselves so that, with confidence, we know where we're headed.

RECALIBRATING YOUR COMPASS

What the hell does this all have to do with courage? Courage is a response tool to move through fear. The most difficult and maybe the least apparent fear to deal with might be to reflect and take an honest look inside of ourselves. It hurts to see what's in there. It hurts to realize that inside, we might be a little ugly at times. Seeing my behavior from an outside perspective and accepting that who I'm trying to project to others and to myself is often compromised, and it stings. But it's precisely what allows me to *actually* become that person I want to be. When I see what I didn't before, and I don't like it, I can't pretend it's not there anymore. I've uncovered something about myself that is holding me back from accomplishing what I actually want. Now I can't blame my circumstances or other people, because I've found something to work on that is fully in my control, which means my difficult circumstance is no longer a stalemate. I have more moves to make, and I can still win. I might have to sacrifice a piece of myself to get there, but it's usually a good move.

It's difficult to make acts of courage if we don't know why we're making them. Dealing with fear and pain has to have some sort of meaning. If you're simply putting yourself through shit for no reason, it's a hard sell, and no wonder you would be more comfortable living with your fears than moving through them if you don't care enough for what is on the other side. It's for this reason that we need to dream. We need to set goals. We need to imagine ourselves as someone bigger than we are. Well-intentioned people will advise you to be happy with yourself and not compare yourself to others—to be happy with what you have and who you are. But we often take the advice out of context. (Those advisors might accidentally be sharing out of context as well.) Dreams and goals should inspire us to grow. People we admire should inspire us to grow, not to feel smaller because we aren't where they are. They give us both an aim and an understanding of specifically *why* that aim matters. This is our compass. It is the magnetic pull that guides the direction of our actions. When things get cloudy and all we can think of at the moment is how to survive, the best strategy is to reflect, recalibrate, and remind ourselves not only of what we're ultimately trying to accomplish, but *why*.

What I realize when I write my letters is that unless I take the time to develop and articulate my point of view, the recipient will not understand what I'm thinking. That's a pretty logical thought. It should be common sense, but common sense is not always common practice—at least it isn't for me every time. I'm full of assumptions because I'm always in my own head, and I forget to differentiate between what I verbalize and what I think. When I write a letter, I need my recipient to understand what I feel about them, what my inner narrative about the situation is, and what I ultimately want to accomplish. It is my responsibility to articulate that, and no one else's. Even if we'd had conversations before about all the issues that came up in our fight, just as my compass could lose calibration, so could theirs. If my thoughts were cloudy, why wouldn't theirs be cloudy as well? It's possible that they might be dealing with twice the shit I am. I often go back to my letters from the past, simply to recalibrate my thoughts. They remind me not only of what I'm trying to accomplish, but also of what I'm capable of overcoming.

Most challenges we have in life that others can see and identify give us the illusion that those challenges are external problems—a physical part of this world. If we choose not to run from or simply live with the issues and instead decide that we actually want to solve the problem, it's no wonder we attempt to do so with external solutions. But the external problem—the one we can see, hear, touch, or measure in some tangible way—is most often a symptom of something internal. It's a projection of what's happening deep within us. That's the fear we need to face. We have to take the internal journey of dealing with our authentic thoughts and emotions, of being real with ourselves, and then of accepting full responsibility for our circumstances before we go out and try to solve the external. Just like we've learned in medicine, treating a symptom (the external) rather than a root cause (the internal), if it works at all, is very likely to come back in another form later. That's when we get tired of life and wonder why the same problems reoccur. This feeling is our prompt to step back, recalibrate our intentions, and take personal responsibility for creating the patterns that continue to reoccur in our lives.

CHAPTER 10

ACCEPTING RESPONSIBILITY

In relationships, it takes more than one person for a conflict to arise. While the other may have the "bigger problem" (they always do, from our point of view, don't they?), if we focus on that, we deflect our own internal issues, essentially ignoring our personal responsibility. With the social media era, we've all been given a voice that is probably too easy to use, as we can hide behind our keyboards, not exposing our true selves and our flaws as we pick and choose what we want to project of ourselves. That makes sense, because why would we expose ourselves to unnecessary judgment? In an effort to connect with our own personal values, we become obsessed with holding everyone accountable for their actions, especially those in leadership or celebrity positions. We start movements by speaking of the injustice done by one person to another, or by exposing a leader for his flaw or his isolated mistake. We romanticize the notion of a world that would work perfectly—if only everyone would comply with *our* world-view, the planet would be healed, pollution would end, and no one would ever offend anyone ever again. That is the utopia we create as we craft our Facebook posts and share videos of the injustices of the world which have nothing to do with us, and we're appalled to think that other humans could do such careless things.

This is only a slight step up from speaking in private to our friends about all the mistakes that our mutual friend is making. I'm not referring to the type of conversation where you're actually trying to help, but the one where it makes you feel good that you have your shit together just slightly better than they do (it's worth asking yourself which you're after when you catch yourself in this situation). We subconsciously put ourselves on a pedestal by shining a light on another's issues, effectively casting a shadow over our own. When attention is directed away from us, we can ignore or even forget the things we're too afraid to deal with ourselves, and no one else will notice either. It's a great plan, as no one will attempt to hold us accountable this way, but if they do, we're thrown into the mix with the rest of society all at the same time. Something about that makes us feel much safer, and yet we're part of a movement in making the world a better place.

When we focus specifically on leaders, prime ministers, presidents, and CEOs—whether with love or hate—we put them on a pedestal and ignore their humanity. No one is perfect. Because they've assumed formal responsibility, they volunteer to demonstrate their humanity by putting themselves under our microscope the moment they sign up to be in our service. They make a mistake, and we jump on it like fleas on a dog. The argument might be that it's important to hold someone with that much power accountable for their actions. Not only are they our role models, but if they can do as they wish without repercussions, they may move further in the direction of their power trips and forget the purpose of their role, which is to serve their country, employees, or fans.

That makes perfect sense; however, it shouldn't stop there. It should act as a trigger for us to look in the mirror and hold ourselves equally accountable for our own behaviors. This is the time where being selfish might be the better solution to our world's problems. If we concerned ourselves with our own personal responsibility above anyone else's, we might become less dependent on our leaders. Realizing our own personal power might cause us to empathize more with those leaders' situations. Then, we could kick the pedestal out from beneath them and realize that we have an equal playing field. Hierarchies are intended to clarify roles and responsibilities for specific goals.

A restaurant needs its dishwasher just as much as it needs

its servers, cooks, manager, and CEO. Every position serves an important purpose, but relinquishing personal responsibility because we aren't at the top of the totem pole ensures that we'll always be dissatisfied. We'll blame our circumstances on our leadership. If you really want to make a difference in the world, work from the inside out. Start with your own work—with your own life. Work on your authentic journey within, and you'll soon notice your own life improving. Then, slowly, you'll notice the world around you getting better. You'll notice your voice will carry much more weight when it's required, because you won't use it to complain, expose, or criticize. You might offer real solutions, and because people will know and feel that you'll back it up with action, they will take notice. No one explains this better than clinical psychologist and psychology professor Jordan B. Peterson, who wrote about this idea in his book *12 Rules for Life: An Antidote to Chaos*. One of his twelve rules is to "set your house in perfect order before you criticize the world." Though many find it controversial, his book provides an eloquent perspective to a deeper comprehension in effecting the change we seek.

BLAME AND HUMILITY

The kindest people I know truly care for the well-being of others. They intuitively know how we feel based on our demeanor, and it's as if our happiness is *their* mission. It's really a beautiful thing to have such people in our lives, if we're fortunate enough. It might be a parent, grandparent, teacher, or friend, and perhaps we might be that person for others. More of us tend to fall into this category as adults caring for children. When we sense vulnerability in a child, we empathize and instinctively want to protect them from their own emotions, but good intentions without careful thought can backfire on us. A safe environment is a legitimate necessity, but in an attempt to create it for those in our care, we might offer them an alibi for their shortcomings.

If a child loses a soccer match, maybe we tell them they should have won, but the referee wasn't fair, or the other players cheated, or their coach called the wrong play—anything to deflect them from being too hard on themselves. We have a bona fide (or biased) alibi for their failed effort, and it frustrates us, perhaps more than it does them. In those instances, the child is an extension of us, and there's no way we're going to let them believe that something out of their control was their own fault. And if it *was* their fault, we won't allow them to hinge any sense of self-worth on this failed attempt.

God forbid they make the same mistake we did, because we know what a terrible feeling that can be. As we empathize with their situation, it brings us back to similar moments in our past that we wish we could forget. In an attempt to spare them from pain, we experiment with kind words and soothing alibis. Then, as we experience the effect we have on them in that moment, we recognize that we've stumbled upon a useful tool that renders us personally responsible for creating positive emotion. Only somewhat consciously, we store this strategy in our tool kit for making others feel better. After all, those of us who have figured out how to create our own happiness know that the best way to do so is to make others happy. So now we offer alibis to others whenever they are down, and it works. But there is one small problem.

When you're deprived of sleep but have to keep going, what do you tend to crave? What is the hardest food to resist in those instances? If you're like most of us, it's sugar and simple carbs. Not only do they taste amazing, but they give us an immediate spike of energy and make us feel full. If we're completely caught up in the moment, it's the perfect remedy for our low energy. However, if we're thinking a few hours into the future, we know that those immediate spikes lead to a hard crash. If we're thinking even farther into the future, we remember that our bodies will store that energy as fat, ultimately making us slower, heavier, and craving more of the same stuff. We ironically become dependent on the very thing that makes us feel worse. Because we love immediate fixes, this creates a vicious cycle of poor nutrition and ultimately hinders our ability to better create our own energy.

But that's future you's problem. Right now, you're tired and just need to feel better. You allow your instincts to guide your decisions because you don't have the energy to battle them in defense of your future self. But what if you held the thought that making the more difficult choice today is an act of love toward your future self? If you work today to make tomorrow a little easier for the future you, the choice in the moment might not require as much energy as you thought. You might choose a different path than the sugar and carbs that would feel so satisfying. Your future self would thank you, as you're responsible for creating better circumstances and ultimately a better environment to live in, one sacrifice at a time.

Offering an excuse, if executed without proper tact, is the equivalent of offering a doughnut to your tired colleague who needs a jolt of energy to keep them going. We've all done it for someone, and someone has done it before for us. If we offer them a narrative that steers their attention away from themselves and toward a problem that simply couldn't be solved, our good intention bestows them instant relief and a cushion to their declining confidence. *The obstacle was the problem, not us.*

This is the reason we're tempted to provide alibis. They accelerate the "feel good" process, which we've tricked ourselves into thinking is the goal. But if we set our sights further into the future, we recognize that obstacles will always stand in the way of our missions. If we train ourselves and others to focus on what is out of our control, we are, in essence, programming ourselves to fail at anything difficult. This is easy to do because we inadvertently become experts in identifying all the reasons it wasn't supposed to work. Just like the insulin spike from sugar, we feel a little better about ourselves and conclude that things "just weren't meant to be." If we're a little more pissed off, we decide that the world has it out for us and success is reserved for the "lucky ones." We conclude that, based on the impossible obstacles placed in our way, we are not one of them.

The well-intentioned attempts to insulate someone from shattering their confidence often come with a side effect that programs us to relinquish personal responsibility. When we believe that other people and obstacles have enough power to determine our fate, we inadvertently allow them to do just that. The belief itself, whether we're still fighting on the outside or not, is the very act of surrendering your power to the obstacle. That's worth reading again: *The belief itself is the very act of surrendering your power to the obstacle.*

THE DANGERS OF PRETENDING

This doesn't mean that self-belief alone will allow you to achieve everything you've ever wanted, but it's an essential ingredient to the recipe. It also doesn't mean that we should naively or overconfidently believe we can achieve anything we want, simply because our thoughts tell us so. Nor should we ignore or pretend that the obstacles aren't actually standing in our way—that might be even more dangerous. When a race car driver loses control on the track, if he wants any chance of recovering, he must keep his eyes and his focus on where he wants the car to go. His instincts will guide the car to do what it needs to regain control, but if he takes his eyes off the road to glance at the wall for even a fraction of a second, he *will* hit the wall. Focusing on what we want steers our attention toward what we're trying to achieve instead of what stands in our way. The race car driver can't blame the wall for being there. He can't blame the road for curving too sharply. He can't blame the other car for cutting him off, either, because it's what he signed up for, and it's what pushes him to get better. If he fails, he doesn't wish for easier competition or a more forgiving track. He uses that moment to teach him, and if he has a winning mentality, he takes full ownership of the situation.

Though it hurts to think about it, he replays the situation over and over in his mind until he figures out a way to do it better next time—to *be* better next time. That exercise hurts in the moment, but it doesn't paralyze him or make him run. It fuels him to become better. But if his pit crew or his family planted the idea that it wasn't his fault, and if he allowed himself to accept that, his growth might stop dead in its tracks. Similar situations would arise again and again, and his frustrations toward this stupid sport would escalate. Soon it wouldn't be fun, and he'd decide that it's time to hang 'em up. "Racing just isn't like it used to be. It's not fun anymore." He'd look for all the reasons that the sport changed and failed him because it would be too painful to accept responsibility for the fact that he stopped trying to be better. The skills were still there, waiting to be developed and improved, but the mindset wasn't. The moment he stopped looking for a way through the challenge, he subconsciously started looking for a way out.

We try to protect the confidence we have by not going too deep within ourselves to uncover and fill the holes of what can be done better, but the irony is that this is precisely the remedy we need in order to boost our skills and strengthen our confidence. Without the willingness to be vulnerable, our confidence is filled with holes that we ignore, which are waiting to sink our ship when the seas get rough and expose our weaknesses, ultimately drowning us in the overwhelming trials of life.

FLUID THINKING

Often there are elements outside of us that need to change in order for us to achieve our goals, but before we let ourselves off the hook, if we're committed to a worthy outcome, we must be careful not to accept that notion too quickly. If

we're part of the process (and we always are), rigid thinking can lead to extreme frustration. When we're attached
to one way of getting to where we want to go, we're more
likely to end our mission in defeat. A hammer knows only
one strategy for getting through a surface. Aesthetically, it
is strong and intimidating. It's a great tool whose approach
often works—as long as the obstacle is a nail or a weaker
surface. But when the hammer meets a surface stronger
than itself, it will continue to pound away and away without making progress because this is all it knows to do.

In this case, we're better served to think of ourselves as
fluid. Water is not quite as intimidating as a hammer, but
as we've all experienced, it is one of the most powerful elements on this planet. A few drops will effect little change,
but continue to pour it over any surface and it will find
its way through the cracks, patiently wearing down the
surface and eventually even remolding the terrain to lead
where it wants to go. This is how our rivers and streams
were built. Melted snow from the mountaintops eventually turned to streams, then waterfalls, then rivers, and in
time, made their way to the ocean, where its true power
is demonstrated.

Being fluid means that when we're trying to achieve something, and our strategy isn't working, we can drop the
hammer and be open to using a new tool. It requires us to
relax our minds and recalibrate our thoughts. We start by

reminding ourselves of what we're truly trying to accomplish, and then we set our focus on the solution rather than the problem. If we remain fixed on the original image of how the process was to look or how we project ourselves to others, we're likely to forget that *we* are the ones who must change in order to defeat the obstacle. If we change our thinking, we can change our strategy, unattached to how we presumed the process should be.

If the obstacle is a relational issue between us and another, and we're fixed on being right or on ensuring that the other side sees our point of view, we'll continue to struggle as if we're pounding one hammer against another. (Spoiler alert: it never works, even when we think we've won.) Our egos take over our ability to reason and deceive us into fighting the wrong battle. Conflict can be a healthy thing and can ultimately lead to the most favorable result, but its purpose is for both parties to open their minds to different points of view. If you're thinking of a personal situation right now and your first thought is, *Yes, exactly! He needs to see my point of view. I already see his and he just won't listen to my side*, then *you* are the problem, not the solution. You are the hammer, not the water. When we've reached this point, we've stopped asking ourselves questions, and we've made up our minds about our direction. This is precisely what the other party is thinking too. It's a stalemate, and nobody wins.

Stephen Covey offers a perfect solution in his book *The 7 Habits of Highly Effective People*. He tells us the fifth habit is to "seek first to understand, then to be understood." If we do that, we take the initiative in defusing a hostile situation. But we can't fake it. We actually have to drop our guard and be completely open to what the other person is suggesting. We have to give the other person complete power for a moment. This is something our egos don't easily surrender to, because it means we have to be open to the possibility that we're wrong. Once the other person feels completely understood, they will feel safe, drop their armor, and try to understand your point. In order to accomplish this, you *must* calibrate your intentions and establish that you're after the same end goal, unattached to how you achieve it or who gets the credit. You must stretch your sights farther into the future.

CHAPTER 11

HUMILITY

At the age of eighteen, I had already been living with my older brother and his friends for quite a while. Justin and his circle of friends seemed to have it all. Most owned their own homes, drove nice trucks, and had *all* the motor toys. They owned dirt bikes, sport bikes, snowmobiles, ATVs, and muscle cars—all the stuff young guys covet. I was barely making ends meet while working as a lot boy at a used car dealership, and I didn't even own a car. I took the bus to work, and I didn't have much more to my name than the clothes on my back. Justin and his friends all worked in the booming oil industry in Alberta. Money attracted me to the industry, but I had no idea what I was getting myself into as Justin found me a position working the sister crew of his drilling rig.

The rig was located in the foothills of Alberta, hours away from any civilization. The work was challenging, with long hours, no breaks, and weeks of isolation as we lived in pop-up camps nearby. Justin had been working on this particular rig for a few years and was very well respected by his coworkers. He was a hard worker and very intelligent. He was mechanically inclined and a great problem-solver. For what Justin contributed to the work, he also contributed to the crew's morale. He knew how to bring joy to an often-unhappy work environment, and perhaps his greatest quality is that he truly cared about getting the best results he could. The crews loved him.

But I was a different story. I didn't fit in, wasn't mechanical, wasn't the hardest worker, and wasn't bringing any joy to anyone. It's not that I didn't want to. I just didn't know how. As an eighteen-year-old kid, I was overwhelmed with the workload, the hours, the seclusion, and just being around certain types of people that I wasn't used to being around. I was thrown into a very unfamiliar world.

In trying to gain the respect that my brother had, I observed and tried to imitate him. Most notably, I tried to imitate his knowledge. I completely ignored the fact that he had several years of experience on me. When I was shown something, I knew Justin would have grasped it right away. Whether I actually grasped what I was shown or not, I pretended I did. I was trying to protect myself from look-ing stupid to others. The irony is that everyone could see right through the façade, and this is precisely what made me look stupid. Part of why Justin so easily understood what he was taught was that when learning, he wasn't focusing on being judged. He asked a lot of questions. He tried to go deeper and deeper by probing and following up the answer to his question with another question. Then he would challenge the other with even more questions, such as "What if this?" or "What if that?" That is how he learned to become a good problem-solver. He worked hard to understand not only how things functioned, but why they worked that way. Then, when a problem arose, he stuck with it long enough to find the solution.

The key to Justin's attitude—and therefore his success—was his humility. He was humble enough to ask questions, learn, and improve. Humility is the remedy to our ego. It's also the magnet that attracts good people and good results to our lives. Internally, we often mistake humility for weakness, as it requires vulnerability and brutal honesty. Our ego can't handle that, as it attempts to protect us from psychological harm, even from ourselves. If we expose ourselves to others, or worse, to ourselves, it feels like we're taking our armor off in the middle of a battle. It feels like the opposite of confidence, but as it turns out, it's precisely the path toward it.

Humility is the ability to see yourself authentically, to recognize both your blemishes and your strengths, and objectively decipher what is needed of you to accomplish your goal, regardless of the feelings it might bring up. It allows you to open your mind and recognize both what you know and what you don't know. If you're too afraid to uncover a weakness, it's wise to remind yourself that you don't *become* your emotions—unless you allow it. The emotions that accompany your thoughts as you uncover a weakness hold no power over you. On the contrary, if you allow yourself to feel whatever comes, without judgment but simply with awareness, you'll experience the very power you're looking for.

One of the greatest gifts we can give to our future selves is to develop our ability to open our minds and see our character as it really is, right in this moment. This doesn't merely serve us well in situations with others, but it allows us to be open to proper learning. If this knowledge had been available to me at that time, my experience in working on a rig would have been completely different.

BECOMING A LIABILITY

I hated every minute of that rigging job, and I think most of the workers hated me too. Nevertheless, I didn't want to leave, because I had put myself in a financial situation where I needed to make the money that only the oil field could provide to an uneducated twenty-one-year-old.

As our rig shut down, Justin and I were separated and sent

to separate parts of the province. He continued to move up the ranks and gain more respect within the company, while I lived miserably, stuck in the same position. A few years later, we were reunited. It was a week to the day after his wedding, and Justin was now the head of his own crew with the position known as the driller, while I was officially awarded the position of his stud roughneck (that's a promotion to second from the bottom). We started our two-week hitch working the night shift, and we'd just moved locations, so our task was to assemble the rig. No drilling happens until the rig is completely set up, so the work in the first week is different. Rather than staying up in his watch spot, called the doghouse, the driller is free to move around and help his hands set up.

On the very first night, I was working alone below the drill floor, when I suddenly heard a loud crash. When anything big gets dropped, we know it's not good news, and the damaged equipment is usually expensive. This time, however, there was more than just damaged equipment. The crash was followed by a loud scream. I dropped my tools and ran over to investigate. I found my brother lying on the floor, with the other crew members watching him in shock. The forks from a front-end loader were dropped, pinning his leg down beneath the heavy steel forks. His leg was amputated later that day.

It was a traumatic experience for all of us. Justin was off

for some time, and as he acquainted himself with his prosthetic, he took an engineering program at a local college and eventually went back to work with the same company. To no one's surprise, he continued to move up the corporate ladder, this time in the office rather than the field. I went back to work the week after the accident, and I remained working with the company for some time. I was even promoted, although it was completely out of pity. Over the next few months, my hatred for the job escalated, and it became increasingly difficult to focus on my tasks while I was on duty. This is not safe when you're working with heavy equipment and moving parts. I started to become a liability to myself and others, constantly making mistakes that would often turn into small injuries.

On one afternoon, I activated a steam line that I knew was frozen. It was a stupid idea, but I thought if it was just a bit of ice blocking the line, I could cheat by letting the pressure from the steam push the ice out of the hose. After all, 100 psi of scorching steam should easily handle a bit of ice. As the pressure built up, steam shot the clogged ice chunk out so hard that I lost control of the hose and it kicked back hard enough to slip through my hands and catch my face. As if getting shot in the face with a chunk of ice didn't hurt enough, the scorching 240-degree Celsius steam following behind it also burned all the hair off the side of my face. I was wearing a safety harness with metal loops near my chest, and the steam heated the metal so high that it burned through my fireproof coveralls, right onto my chest. I had a hard time hiding that one, but somehow I got away with keeping my job for a while longer.

Three months later, I was fired. I couldn't see it at the time, but it was the best thing that ever happened to me. It might have even saved my life.

CHASING THE WRONG RABBIT

I knew I hated that job. I knew I wasn't good at it, and I knew I should have left, but I felt stuck. I had started a business a few years earlier that failed miserably, leaving me with a massive pile of debt. I had the choice to stick out the oil field job while I paid down my debt, or I could file for bankruptcy. Looking back on it now, I see there were so many lessons I learned there that helped me become who I am—someone I'm truly proud of. But in the moment, any shred of confidence I had before working in the oil field was completely crushed by that job.

It was incredibly humbling to spend three out of four weeks in the middle of nowhere with a small crew of people, doing something I was terrible at. My boss hated me, my coworkers thought I was stupid and lazy, and those very same people thought the world of my brother. Getting fired hurt. I was embarrassed having to explain myself to others at home, and I knew I couldn't make something up. I also felt rejected and confused about my next steps. At the same time, I felt tremendous relief leaving an environment that I knew had run its course.

Still, fifteen years later, whenever I'm stressed about my current business, I go to sleep and live a recurring dream that I'm headed back to work on drilling rigs. It's funny how the human mind works, but it gets me thinking. There isn't a chance in hell I would ever go back, but if I did, I *know* with all conviction that I would be great at it. Why? Because I learned about humility. The thing that made me bad at that job was my ego. I tried to protect my confidence by projecting an image of how I wanted to be seen—smart and competent. Ironically, that strategy was responsible for keeping me from actually becoming smart and competent. Had I adopted Justin's curious qualities and not worried about being judged for my questions, my crew would have happily worked with me to deepen my understanding of the work. I would have built up my knowledge, my aptitude, and my confidence. The dynamics with my coworkers would have been completely different.

Instead, I concluded that they were all jerks, the work sucked, and I just didn't have what it took. I decided my brother was "the lucky one." I thought he was destined for greatness, and I was destined for a mediocre career and a miserable life. This is the trick our ego plays on us. It is crucial that we're aware of what we're actually chasing. All too often, we're after the by-product of success. We don't realize that someone's actual success is in becoming the person who emanates on the inside what the rest of us see on the outside. When we deny our vulnerability, we instead project an image of how we want others to see us. The more we're tested, the harder it is to fake. We think we're playing this great trick on the world, when in reality, most see us in a much clearer light than we do. Chasing external success rather than going deep blocks us from becoming the very person we want to become.

ACCEPTING RESPONSIBILITY IS NOT ACCEPTING BLAME

When my two boys were younger and had an issue with each other, frustrations would grow, and it would turn into a fight. Defeated in realizing it wouldn't end without help from their parents, one would make their way to me or their mom, and the other would follow. Both would be hell-bent on convincing us of who was at fault for creating the conflict. One would exclaim, "He started it!" The other would reply, "No! He did this." Then the other would predictably refute, "Yeah, but he did that." If you're a parent, I'm sure this sounds familiar. Neither wants to be blamed for what happened, and if only one gets in trouble, it's difficult for him to take. He's programming himself to believe that the world is against him and life isn't fair—at least not for him, because the other played a significant role in provoking, and once they felt a certain way, they surrendered to their emotional reactions. They think, *If someone makes me mad, it's their fault if I retaliate. I'm just trying to protect myself.* This is something we expect in kids, as we know they're learning with each trial, and it's up to the parents to help them understand the dynamics of self-control and proper human interaction. Children are also gifted with being much more present in each moment than we are as adults, but being fully present in moments of conflict creates an added challenge, as they wrap themselves deeply into the situation. Nothing matters more to them than being understood. If we can somehow help them accomplish this, it's the remedy that begins to release their frustrations and moves them toward a solution (at least until the next conflict).

As adults, we assume we've matured past this stage, as if our emotional maturity automatically keeps pace with our physical maturity. We're certainly less likely to resort to violence, and we're more skilled at articulating our issue with words. However, there's much more to maturing than an expanded vocabulary and physical restraint. When we're engaged in a debate, are we actually listening to the other side and trying to see their point, or are we focused on proving them wrong so we can be right? We can easily identify immaturity in other adults when we're engaged in conflict, but we hardly ever see it in ourselves. (This sounds awfully similar to children's conflicts, doesn't it?)

If we want evidence, we only need to go as far as our Facebook and Twitter feeds or to listen to our politicians "debate" for five minutes. We constantly try to teach our kids not to engage in destructive behavior with their friends and siblings, yet we demonstrate the opposite in our own approach to life. This is the classic case of blindly advising to "do as I say, not as I do." Have we actually tricked ourselves into believing that, as adults, we're dealing with more trivial issues than children are, and therefore the solution to our problems is somehow different than the solution to theirs? Ironically, the strategy we use to "solve" our problems happens to be the very *cause* of the unproductive conflict that we identify in our children.

CHANGING THE NARRATIVE

When a group project (I use that term broadly) goes badly, what is our narrative? What story do we tell ourselves and others about how and why things went the way they did? We might look internally and feel good about our personal effort. Maybe the problem was that another person involved didn't fulfill their responsibility, or maybe something unexpected came out of nowhere to derail our plan. Perhaps the person on the other side of the table "just doesn't get it." Maybe their ego is too big, and they don't care about the bigger picture.

We might be right about all those things, but the trouble

with sticking to that narrative is that it doesn't offer a solution. It only offers a reason to be frustrated and ultimately serves as an excuse that either soothes our agony or fuels our anger on the road toward failure. The catastrophe, however, is rarely the failure of accomplishing our goal. It is the missed opportunity for growth, as there's always a great lesson that hides in the shadow of our excuses. Just as our children can't see past the heated moment that wraps their entire being into this single conflict, we also forget that we have plenty of life left to live, and this goal is simply one experience in the grand scheme of our life's journey. Paradoxically, how we handle this particular conflict influences the path to our success. Therefore, the mission might be as important as we give it credit, but not for the reason we assume.

The ultimate goal is to grow as a person, and with each experience, we learn something that makes us better for the next one. We can't expect our results to change a whole lot if *we* don't change. We'll always encounter a crisis that reminds us that life isn't fair or that other people are short-sighted and selfish. (Never us, though, right?) If we're too wrapped up in the moment, our focus shifts from solving the actual problem that we originally intended, toward solving a different problem, which is to be "right." This is our ego's attempt to be understood.

There's far more personal growth involved in failure

than there is in winning. We certainly don't want to fail intentionally, as that would counteract our genuine effort, denying us the very growth we're after. We need wins, and the moment we learn to release all blame, we'll see them come in droves (although I caution you not to be attached to how the "win" appears). With each moment that our focus is set on people or events outside of our control or on casualties of life's forces that oppose our efforts, we give up our personal power, and we fulfill the prophecy of our own narrative.

We love to indulge in movies, books, and real-life hero stories of people who defied all the odds, because they shine a light on our realization that we're all capable of so much more than we give ourselves credit for. I'm not aware of a single story that inspires us in this way where there was no adversity, no pain, and no failure. It wouldn't be much of a story in that case. Yet, when it comes to our own personal story, we're so quick to condemn the shit that's thrown at us, when the shit is the very thing that gives us an opportunity to become heroes ourselves. Heroes move their way through the impossible because their mission has enough meaning that it allows them to do so. The desire to succeed outweighs the sacrifice they must make, and they accept taking the risk that they might lose more than they started with.

Finding meaning is a little easier when someone else's life

is at stake or our country's fate is clearly in our hands, as we might see in a movie. It doesn't make the mission easier, but it makes the "why" crystal clear. To give meaning to our own suffering requires a lot of energy, and no one is asking us to do it. Yet if we dig deep and articulate the real "why" for our goals, we clarify our aim and find a reason to carry on. When we have an aim, we have a direction, and we're less likely to be distracted by the forces that threaten our ego. We don't allow ourselves to be distracted into satisfying our immediate personal needs (which are usually related to comfort), because we hold on to our understanding that the mission is more important than those needs, and it is well worth the sacrifice.

CHAPTER 12

RESPONSE-ABILITY

I've always been infatuated with Navy SEALs—men and women of the US Navy's primary special operations force— as they're some of the toughest people on the planet, both mentally and physically. Naturally, when choosing books to read, I'm drawn to those written by SEALs, as I know they are the real deal. They live a life that is less common to us and more akin to our ancestors, when our world was a more violent and dangerous place. Yet the characteristics they require for success are the very same we could use to succeed in modern civilization. It's just not as "in your face" without the bombs and the guns. Our battles are subtler, and they're drawn out over longer periods. If we refuse to see them as such or to ignore them altogether, it's easy to dismiss what's required of us to succeed. But make no mistake—every goal, wish, or dream will be met with opposition, and therefore, it is a battle.

SEALs require courage, discipline, fortitude, grit, preparation, and the ability to work together. The "why" in their mission is about the care of others before themselves. Most of all, those who thrive in the SEAL environment practice *Extreme Ownership*. This is the title of a book written by Jocko Willink and Leif Babin, two retired Navy SEALs who are now leadership consultants in the business world. Their book speaks of real-life missions in Ramadi, Iraq, some of which went wrong. Passing the blame to a subordinate for the failed missions could easily be warranted if they shared the mentality most of us do, but these leaders always took full ownership of their missions. They held themselves fully accountable, and that created a safe environment where their subordinates almost couldn't help but look in the mirror and hold themselves to the same standard. They understood that passing blame doesn't increase the chance of a better outcome on the next mission. When others' lives are at stake, there's no space or time to blame any other, and there's no option to leave the outcome to chance. They would never concede failure when the enemy has better odds, because winning is the only option. The single approach they used—and still use—to hold power was to look in the mirror and ask what they could adjust in themselves.

When I read stories like the ones from that book, I can't help but look in the mirror and ask myself, *When do I neglect to fully own the outcomes in my life?* When a business venture is failing, it's too easy to become frustrated at the other people involved, as I might fix my attention on others' problems. I might concern myself with those who don't take it as seriously as I do, or who see a different vision and are rigid in their ideas, or maybe those whom I deem to have less talent. Perhaps it's a little more difficult to focus on the true mission because there's substantially less at stake than in a military operation. While SEALs are often risking human life, I'm risking money. The concept of money is simply a story we tell ourselves, one in which we often embellish its importance. If I make the comparison through this lens, I have to concede that my situation is substantially easier. I have to remind myself not to take my mission too seriously and to treat it more like a game. But I can still adapt SEAL principles, accepting only what I can do differently to influence the outcome I'm looking for. I can stop wishing things were different or lamenting that they aren't easier. And the moment I do, I gain the clarity to see things as they really are. This allows me to get to work on making the right things happen.

THE ABILITY TO RESPOND

When we break down life's challenges to their root, they're all people challenges. A Navy SEAL on a mission faces layers of them. The obvious one is the enemy—people with an opposing mission. The SEAL needs to dig deep to plan, train, and execute if he is to beat them. The other people challenges are found in his superiors and subordinates. He needs to communicate clearly with each one so they fully understand the mission and their role within it because nobody can win on their own. Then there are the physical obstacles that can get in their way, like the terrain, the elements, the bombs, and the bullets. These aren't directly people issues, but the soldier himself is a person. Therefore, it's an internal challenge. He needs to be alert, agile, physically capable, and so much more. All those points could be expanded upon, but if he's to succeed, it all breaks down to his internal ability to respond. Put another way, he must understand and accept his *response-ability*.

I sell real estate for a living. It's much less badass than a Navy SEAL's job but, nonetheless, I try to adapt their principles to my work. When I advise a client on selling their home, I might suggest items to prepare in order to maximize the property's salability. I will also suggest where to set the optimal asking price to maximize the end result. It's human nature that we all want the most for the least, and most of us tend to want to try for a higher sale price. Therefore, it's natural and common that the homeowner doesn't want to accept my advice. Living and breathing real estate for fifteen years and being involved in thousands of transactions has afforded me the experience to know that pricing too high works against us the great majority of the time. If the homeowner doesn't accept my advice, I can leave it at that and then complain to my fellow realtors when the house isn't selling, holding on to my story that the client was unreasonable and it's not my fault that the home hasn't sold because he didn't take my advice. Or worse, the client might interview other agents until he finds one agreeable enough to list the property at the higher price; then I lose the client altogether. I might think, *People are so stupid! I told them what they needed, and now they aren't getting their results. I told them, but nobody listens in this business.*

If this is my attitude, my real estate career will be mediocre to average at best. I'd need to play the numbers game: I'd lose many deals, and every so often, I'd work with someone reasonable enough who required less influence to take my advice. I'd have to work harder, constantly looking for more clients because I'd need to find and take more appointments to close one sale.

CHANGING THE LENS

What if I looked at obstacles through a different lens? The obstacle is that the homeowner doesn't agree that my strategy is the best one for him. Why? Perhaps it's because I haven't articulated it well enough, or perhaps I haven't given him the space to fully articulate his point of view. *I tried my best. Maybe he just wasn't the right fit for my personality. Maybe I'm attracting the wrong clients. Where are all the nice people who just "get" me?* If this is my train of thought, I'm asking the world to conform to me instead of molding myself to work within the world I live in.

When I realize that I need to better articulate and empathize with others, I've identified an area where I can train myself. Articulating verbally isn't my natural strength. So I write in order to clarify my thoughts. I can practice writing an explanation of my pricing strategy, then practice speaking it until I develop my ability to articulate my case. If that still doesn't work for the next sales call, I need to look deep within to see what other problems there are that I'm not accepting. Perhaps the clients don't trust me. I need to make sure I'm *earning* their trust, and I only have a few minutes to accomplish this. How do I do that? I need to establish two types of trust with clients. There's trust in my character—knowing that I have their very best interests in mind as I give my advice—and there's trust in my competence as a realtor—that I know the market and I know how to get the job done. The two don't always work hand in hand. They are separate issues, and in order to earn both types of trust, I need to take a deep look at myself and ensure I actually deserve it. Am I as competent as I think I am? Are my intentions to help them as pure as I tell myself they are?

Establishing trust in my competence is tricky because my confidence is fleeting. It moves up and down, and when it's down, I don't give myself enough credit. When it's sky-high, I probably give myself too much credit. Before I dissect my ability, I need to be aware of where my confidence is sitting in that moment. I need to remind myself that my client will only have as much confidence in me as I have in myself. Therefore, preparation is the key. I must give myself adequate time to prepare before an appointment and make sure that I think through the client's situation. I have to study the comparables and the market, and if a previous sale or an active listing throws me off, I can make a phone call to the agent involved and ask questions to clarify the situation. Once I've addressed every issue, I can then walk into my meeting with full confidence in my advice. But I'm not ready yet. I need to make sure they trust my character as well. How do I do that?

Before I walk into that appointment, I need to check in with myself on what my intentions are. Am I going in there to "get the listing," to seal the deal on hitting my monthly sales target, or to impress my team members? Those intentions are all about me. If the clients are intuitive, they might read that, and they may not care, as long as it serves their goal as well. But if they value relationships more, that might turn them off. Even if I demonstrate my competence and knowledge, and I articulate my strategy perfectly, that little feeling they get in their gut might tell them not to trust me in assisting with their decisions. The feeling in their gut is that my goal isn't aligned with theirs.

They may not feel like I understand them or that I care enough to give them the advice that is in *their* best interest.

How do I get myself to care more about their goal than mine? I need to care about who they are. If I haven't met them, I need to get to know them and be curious about what's important to them. Earlier in my career, I'd made myself so busy that my primary goal was time efficiency. In my mind, I needed to get in and out so I could get to my next appointment. I would introduce myself and get straight to the point, as there was no time to talk about anything but the sale. I certainly cared about the best outcome for each client, but I wouldn't take the time to get to know them and their situations. It served me well enough, but when I stumbled onto the power of being fully present with clients and asking more questions, everything changed.

BUILD YOUR AWARENESS

Reflecting on our response-ability is a regular practice. A work situation like the one just described might be the pressing situation in our lives where it's obvious that we want better results, so we might start there. When we discover where we can adapt and evolve ourselves to better influence outcomes, we must follow through on the work that needs to be done. Eventually, we'll benefit from our labor and efforts. Then, with each win, we increase the comprehension of our personal power. Now that we realize our power in that circumstance, it would be wise to reflect on our personal response-ability in other areas of our lives.

As you reflect on how you would like things to be with your relationships, work, finances, and health, break down the big situations into micro-situations and slowly build your awareness of what you can personally do to influence each outcome. Start with what is most pressing—whatever you're least satisfied with in life—and turn it into a project. Once you've built a new habit of behavior, those better results will come easier, and you can move on to the next project of improvement. Eventually, you will see each moment differently, as you'll be aware of your world—not just how you fit into it, but how easily you can alter its outcomes.

Think of our response-ability as a muscle. As we challenge ourselves to improve it, the muscle grows stronger. It can almost become addictive, but we are products of our environments, and it's easy to slip back into frustration with other people. Once you discover your personal power, it's easy to forget that most others aren't aware of their own. Observing their behavior can slowly lead us to an illusion of superiority (masked to us as concern for the other). What is obvious to you isn't always obvious to another. We all arrive at our own pace.

If your conflict or challenge is relational (which, as I

pointed out earlier, it always is), you must bring yourself back to center. If you go so deep into personal ownership that it becomes difficult to empathize with another who hasn't yet discovered what you have, you might accidentally end up fooling yourself into blaming the other person for not accepting their response-ability. This is a significant paradox.

If you've ever played *Pac-Man*, you'll recall that you have to move your character across the screen while picking up the dots for points. As you continue moving him across the screen toward the right, once he passes the edge of the screen, he ends up back on the left, as if it's a continuous loop.

This is what can happen to you if you become overfocused on personal response-ability. Before you know it, you end up in frustration, watching others in their situation. You've worked hard on your own problems, and you understand very well the power that each of us has in creating our own outcomes. When you study another person's problems, do you believe it is your responsibility to tell them their problems are their own fault? If you follow this plan, whom are you focused on? You might inadvertently end up right back where you started.

This is the time to remind yourself of what is in your control and what is not. If you truly care and your intentions are in the right place, remember that good intentions don't always equate to good results. For us to discover our personal power, we can't be *told* by another, especially while we're in a state of frustration. If I haven't sold you on this, try telling your spouse that they are "overreacting" in the midst of your next conflict and see how well it works. (I'm kidding, of course. Don't actually try this. It's a trap!) We need a safe environment to learn this message on our own terms. This is why reading a book or listening to a podcast can be so powerful. The author and speakers are given the space to speak freely without judgment, and we, the audience, listen quietly. We don't listen with the intent to speak back and respond, and this act allows us to open our minds to new philosophies. If we want to help others do the same, we can't simply tell them what to think. If we want to be truly effective, we must learn to influence.

CHAPTER 13

INFLUENCE

———

Water is one of the most important elements we need for life. In fact, it makes up roughly 60 percent of our bodies. Most of us should drink more than we do, as it cleanses us of toxins, keeps us hydrated, helps with weight loss, and does so much more. Nobody disputes its benefits, but if we consume too much water, we will literally drown. Whether we try to drink too much, too fast or we jump into a pool and stop swimming, when water is all that surrounds us, it blocks the other vital elements from reaching us. Then, the very thing that offers us life takes it away. The same is true for the great qualities we hold and develop.

Effective influence requires complete detachment. If we're rigid in producing a specific outcome that involves another person (especially if the outcome we're after is *for* that person), we'll become frustrated when she doesn't behave the way we think she should. If she feels threatened, the ego emerges, protecting her idea at all costs. True change of thought must come on our own terms, and we need to feel safe in order to do so. Therefore, when we're imposing *our* will on another, we're more likely to push the results away than to achieve them. If our goal is to help someone, we're better served to guide them in the discovery of what *they* are after, rather than assuming that we know what they want and telling them what they must do.

Rational or not, we continue to be surprised when someone is behaving improperly. If we're in the right frame of mind, it's difficult to empathize with them, as we don't account for their own internal battles and fears. It's helpful to remind ourselves that we will never get the best out of someone unless *we* are being our best. If we aren't open to what our best truly is within each interaction, how can we expect the best out of the other person? Regardless of how strong our personalities are, we all mirror each other at various degrees, and the more we accept the person for exactly who they are, the safer that person feels. It's worth noting that this cannot be faked. It's at this point when we can create safe environments to discuss a different philosophy in thinking. With no attachment to whether they'll accept it or not, we're much more likely to be effective if we *share* an idea rather than teach it. This is a good time to remind ourselves that the only power that truly belongs to us is the control over our own behavior. An attempt to control anything or anyone else will manifest the very opposite result.

LIFE REQUIRES BALANCE

Just as water offers you life, yet too much of it will take it all away, your greatest strength can become your greatest weakness if overused. Life is a series of learning experiences, and as we experiment with our behavior, we eventually realize that everything requires balance. If humility is your strength, it may be responsible for many great things in your life, but take it too far and it can rob you and others of opportunities, as you forget to acknowledge and lean in to your strengths. If strong will and determination are your strengths, take them too far and you might quit too late on something that you should stop doing, because whether you believe it or not, quitting is sometimes the stronger move. If openness and honesty are your strengths, you may overshare at times and hurt yourself or others.

For this reason, reflection and awareness are incredibly important. We need to understand when we're helping our cause and when we're hurting it. No matter how beneficial a character trait can be, there is a line to cross that takes us too far, and no one else can find that line but *you*. Just as you can't hire someone else to do your push-ups for you and expect your own muscles to strengthen, you cannot engage someone to do your thinking for you. However, just as you can hire a trainer to make sure your physical exercise is on the right track, you can engage someone to help with your thinking and make sure you're asking the right questions. This can come in the form of mentors, psychologists, or coaches, but it can also come from reading books and listening to good podcasts. Just remember, the work still depends on you taking action, and there's no escaping that work if you truly want to improve the results in your life. In the meantime, if you want to keep it simple, ask yourself this question on a constant basis: *Is this serving me?*

IS THIS SERVING ME?

If you're a hard worker, no one will ever dispute the nobility of that trait. It's something we should all strive for. But have you ever forgotten to relax and take yourself less seriously, working past the point of burnout, where you became less and less effective in your work? Hard work serves you well until it doesn't. Does it serve you to keep going? If you take a twenty-thousand-foot view, you might conclude that working hard still serves you, but so does a balance of regular breaks, along with some form of play. My natural disposition is to run until I'm completely gassed. Then, until I can carve out time to get away for a long period, I become less effective in my work and less tolerant with my family. My hard work serves me well, until it doesn't. My personal play and break time activities are parkour, guitar, writing, and daily workouts. (Yes, I consider that play.) It took me years to figure out that when I carve time out for each of these activities in my day, my stamina, morale, and effectiveness—both in my business and as a dad—are significantly increased. I don't need weeklong breaks from work nearly as often because I take micro-breaks.

If you're strong-willed like me (that's the nice way of saying stubborn), some may see it as negative, and others may see it as positive, and they're both right. Strong will allows us to fix our focus on what we want without being too easily swayed. It allows us to keep moving when we're in pain and keeps us from shifting our opinions and thoughts so abruptly that we confuse ourselves and others. A strong will also keeps us from admitting when we're wrong. It prevents us from being open to better ideas, and it might project us as more abrasive toward other humans. Ask yourself when it's serving you and when it opposes the very results you're truly after. Strong will serves me well, until it doesn't. The same can be said for being open-minded. The benefits and challenges of being open-minded are the perfect opposite of the benefits and challenges of being strong-willed.

The list of personal traits that benefit us but can be taken too far can go on forever. The use of comedy is a great way to bring people together and take ourselves less seriously (until we need to get to work and take ourselves more seriously). The left in politics is a great ideal in inclusion and fairness and leaving no one behind (until we over-include, and fairness becomes an unfair advantage). The right in politics is a great ideal in encouraging industrious behavior and autonomy (until our focus blinds us from those who genuinely need help). Loving care and attention to our children is a necessity in fostering their growth (until we forget to give them the autonomy to figure things out alone, to fail, and to get hurt—as we try to protect them from the world, we fail in allowing them to develop into people who are well equipped to deal with the world).

Choose your topic, and we can make a case for its benefits and its curses. Much of the disagreements in the world are based on our thought that everything we believe is either right or wrong. But the world isn't black and white. It's full of color, layers, and a multitude of dimensions. We're programmed to believe that it has to be either/or, and as we fight to prove ourselves right and the other wrong, our egos put up armor in an attempt to defend us from the threat of an opposing view. We then crank up the offense, moving ourselves farther away from being open to the idea that the truth typically lies near the middle of both arguments. And why wouldn't we? We know we're right. We always are. Aren't we?

APPRECIATING OPPOSITES

Nothing exists without its opposite. Without up, down doesn't exist. Without left, we wouldn't understand right.

Without darkness, light isn't relative. Just as if we knew nothing of light, darkness wouldn't exist because light is all we would know. We wouldn't know that we know it without a contrast, because it would simply *be*. Our minds would have no reason to give it awareness. Dating back to at least 600 BC, the Chinese theorized the concept of yin and yang. Picture a circle that is half white and half black, but not divided in a straight line—more like two teardrops that meet to form a perfect circle. One side represents feminine energy and the other masculine energy. When you look closer, there's another white circle within the black section and a black circle within the white section. This represents the balance of the world and the idea that both energies are useful at different times.

For this reason, we know that opposites attract. Deep down, we know that we need balance, and when we're in the company of a different energy, both sides can benefit, though it can be a challenge at times as we attempt to integrate. Our subconscious knows that we need to challenge our tendencies. If we don't expose ourselves to the other side on a continuous basis, we lean more and more to one side, until it stops benefiting our cause and starts to destroy it. It works this way on an individual level, but also as a group, a community, and a country. This is why we see revolutions and extreme ideals sway from one end to the next over the years. When we take a wonderful ideal too far, the other side can easily make a case for why it's destroying us. Like the pendulum paperweight that your grandfather might have kept on his desk, we swing hard to the left until we get too far, then momentum swings in the exact opposite way to counteract, and then we swing all the way back in the other direction until it goes too far. The battle continues, never resting at center for very long unless we physically stop the momentum. In life, however, we rarely bother stopping, as we get lost in the passion of the battle toward either extreme. (Read this paragraph again and think of the battle between left and right politics in your area, as an example.)

We probably shouldn't stop it, either, because if the pendulum stops and we create a perfectly balanced center, we stop moving, and life gets less exciting. We miss opportunities to be challenged, to learn, and to grow, which are really the beautiful things about life and, in my opinion, the whole point. This is why we're here! With this knowledge, it's easier to step back and see life's situations for what they are. Whether it's an internal battle, a conflict between two people, or a divided nation with opposing ideals, we can remove ourselves from our emotions and appreciate the beauty within the chaos of trying to accomplish a balance. When we're aware of this, we might allow ourselves to become a little less offended, a little less shocked, and hopefully wrap ourselves up into the emotions that conflict creates less. If we see the reality from a twenty-thousand-foot view, we can bring awareness to which behavior better serves our cause. As we bring a more peaceful approach to the search for equilibrium, we can better influence the outcome.

The mark of true intelligence is when a person can simultaneously hold two opposing views. We cannot influence others properly until we can influence ourselves, and we cannot properly influence ourselves until we can appreciate the validity of both sides in opposition. If we lower our guard and allow ourselves to truly consider the opposing view, we create a safe environment for the other side to do the same. This happens because humans tend to mirror each other, and this is why we must, as Stephen Covey perfectly stated, "seek first to understand, then to be understood."

To grow our self-assurance requires us to build trust in ourselves. To build trust in ourselves, we need to know that we can be effective in influencing outcomes in our lives. To be effective in influencing outcomes in our lives, we need to work on mastering our emotions, and to master our emotions, we need to be able to separate ourselves from each situation—to see reality for what it is, remove our biases, and rewrite the narrative. When we can appreciate the challenges of life and remove ourselves from our situation, we begin to see the truth in how our behavior affects outcomes and thus the direction of our lives. Understanding what is in our control and accepting what is not paradoxically gives us the power to influence life as we awaken and accept our personal responsibility. Put simply, stop your focus on the external, and you'll quickly experience a shift from a victim of life to a victor of life. If you do this, you won't just enjoy the ride; you might even come to be excited about it and delight in the future you're creating.

CHAPTER 14

SHY AND AWKWARD

———

The reason I became obsessed with the topic of self-assurance is because I was timid. I despised interacting with others and constantly feeling like a lesser person. I despised making a statement and incessantly wondering what others were thinking. I felt like my every word and thought was being judged. I couldn't stand having others' attention, feeling completely exposed when eyes were on me, as I revealed how unsure I was of myself. Each time I encountered a social interaction, I couldn't help but tell myself, *They think I'm full of shit and I don't really know what I'm talking about.* The truth, as I later figured out, is that it wasn't judgment I was feeling, but pity that was caused precisely *because* of my doubt. Who I am and what I know or don't know are inconsequential, but the energy I project is precisely what is felt.

Thankfully, my natural tendency is not to run and hide

from what I don't like. I battle the things that make me uncomfortable until I become comfortable. Fear should never have so much power over us that it robs us from truly living. If we don't work on defeating fear, we become slaves to it and constantly shift our direction, running away each time we come to face it. The challenge with that strategy is that no matter which direction we go, fear will find a way to jump right back in front of us. Our world will continue to shrink, and we'll eventually run out of space and directions to avoid it. The more we run toward comfort, the more uncomfortable life becomes, which, ironically, is the very opposite of our objective. To expand our space and freedom is to battle through our self-imposed limitations using the weapon of courage and learning to be comfortable in discomfort.

Anytime I encountered the feeling of inadequacy, I used someone I admired as inspiration for how I wanted my audience to respond to whatever I was up to, but it never worked. For example, my brother could act silly, and he would elicit laughter from the others. I would attempt the same, and I, along with everyone else, would feel awkward. A friend would inspire and create aha moments as he spoke eloquently to others, and that's what I attempted to recreate. Only no one ever got it, and the situation became awkward. I couldn't figure it out, and every time it happened, my sense of confidence compressed. Inspired by successful musicians or speakers, I built out these dreams of performing, whether it was playing music or speaking. In my mind, the performance would go off without a hitch, but in the real attempts, it never turned out that way. It almost always ended up in that uncomfortable place where my audience didn't know how to react. How could I take the very same actions and even say the very same words as someone else yet elicit a completely different reaction?

VALIDATION

Somewhere along the way, I learned the value of asking questions. I asked questions of people I admired to learn how they defeated their own insecurities (which, in itself, is an act of courage that sparked a solution to the very question). I had once hired an incredible musician named Paul Woida to perform at a client appreciation event that I was hosting for my real estate business. In all of my experiences, I had never seen so many people captivated by one performer, especially in a social setting where the intention was not to focus on the music but to have it as a background as people mingled, ate, and drank. My guests would stop dead in the midst of conversation, turn their heads, and appreciate each moment of his performance. His talent was undeniable, but there had to be more to our infatuation than his voice and musical abilities.

I wanted to get to know him more. I needed to understand who he was and why he was so magnetic. By this time, I'd grown out of my shyness (my real estate business forced much of that out of me), and I asked Paul to meet me for lunch the following month. We agreed to meet at a trendy spot downtown called Rostizado, and Paul arrived before me. The moment I sat down at that table and asked him how he was doing, the floodgates were opened. Without any reservation, he shared much of who he really is, what he was going through, what his dreams were, and the challenges he had in reaching them. He condensed twenty years of getting to know someone well inside of twenty minutes. I'd met people who were comfortable being open before, but this felt different. He wasn't pouring his baggage out in desperation for someone to rescue him. He was at peace but still seeking answers and open to possibilities. If this hadn't been the case, I would have been pushed away, but it was quite the opposite. He drew me in.

The conversation flowed for hours as we discussed music, life, love, and business. I mentioned, toward the end of our conversation, that I played music myself. His vulnerability created a safe environment for me to do the same. With that, I shared that I was terrified of playing in public, and for as much as I loved to play, everything was easier when I was alone. Whenever I built up the courage to play in front of others, that same awkwardness would always come back. The movement of my fingers would turn rigid and unnatural. I would forget lyrics, and suddenly all I would feel was the heat in my face from blood rushing through in embarrassment. That awful pity that I felt from others would return, almost every time.

Paul's response was this: "Never look to the crowd for validation. They're looking for *you* to set the energy, the tone, and the mood."

Sometimes, we receive a message at the very moment we're ready for it, and this particular one would profoundly change my life. It's exactly what I was doing, not simply in music, but in speaking and in almost all my interactions. *They* feed off of *your* energy first, not the other way around. When I began to speak or play, I wouldn't lean in to the tone I meant to set, but I would sort of dip my toes in and look to others to give me some type of signal that they were enjoying it. On occasion, I would get that signal, but then I was stuck there, hoping for them to continue to give me more validation until I literally drove it away, and it turned to awkwardness. My inhibitions were never released, and I wouldn't free myself up to let loose, open up, and lose myself in my craft. This contradicted the very thing I was after.

GIVE VERSUS GET

It's common for empathic introverts to be more than just aware of others in our company. We're also concerned with their thoughts. This is, perhaps, why I love to write. I can more easily release my apprehensions as I sit with my own thoughts and let my mind type freely without reservation. When I write, I can stop thinking about *me*. I can allow myself to forget about "third person" Jeremy, and my problem suddenly becomes clear. If I compare my teenaged self to my present self, the severity has significantly softened over the years, but the moments that didn't go my way were in direct correlation with the moments where I overfocused on myself. Fucking ego! We always tend to associate ego with those who are pompous, loud, and extroverted, but it's just as present for those of us who are quiet and shy. It just projects itself in a different manner. In this case, when I'm wondering what other people are thinking of me, or hoping they will give me validation, I'm trying to *get* something rather than to *give* something, and that very act is the reverse direction of the energy that both sides are after.

Now that I'm aware of this, I can work on changing it. But just because I know doesn't make it an easy task. I have to break a habit I've created and surrendered to throughout my entire life, all while figuring out how to master the strongest opposition there is—the ego. If I'm not actively intentional about battling it, I surrender yet again to this pattern, and I recreate those awkward moments as I shrink inside. Spending time with people who have no trouble being vulnerable and sharing their authentic selves without concern of judgment helps me to break that pattern. Paul's ability to share his vulnerabilities at that lunch meeting drew me to him, and it's precisely the reason that his audience was so captivated when he performed. When he was singing, he wasn't sharing his personal story in words but rather with his soul, baring it to his audience without any reservation. Every note he hit carried unreserved emotion, whichever one was required of the song.

This is a difficult thing to do, though it creates an inner freedom and is probably the reason actors and musicians fall in love with their crafts. To allow ourselves to feel anything, no matter who is watching, requires the willingness to be vulnerable. In this manner, being vulnerable is synonymous with authenticity. Authenticity is what we're attracted to, and we can't be authentic while we shield others and ourselves from what we're feeling or what we want (or don't want) to feel. The ability to acknowledge all our emotions is the very source of true strength. It's the only way to become truly confident.

AUTHENTICITY

Authenticity takes courage when we aren't used to it. It's especially difficult for those who were raised to believe that fear and insecurity are weaknesses and we should never expose them. The contradiction with that logic is that pretending to ourselves and others that it's not present allows it to grow, and if we never face it, we never defeat it. Too often, I've seen this approach lead to depression, addiction, and sadly, suicide—even within my own family. When we're honest with ourselves and acknowledge even the slightest emotion without judgment of whether it's warranted or not, we don't seem to mind it as much. When we're open, we realize that everyone else, or at least those who are honest with themselves, feel all the same stuff that we do. Therefore, there's never a reason to be ashamed. This is why we're drawn to authentic people. We're social beings, and regardless of our personality types, we cannot win some inner challenges by ourselves. Sometimes, just knowing that our emotions aren't unique to us is enough to heal the negative ones, and they dissipate on their own. With this practice, we eventually become comfortable with whatever we're feeling. We become, in essence, *secure*.

SHIFTING FOCUS

When my self-focus becomes excessive, it is generally sparked by a fear. When my confidence lacks, I overfocus on myself. In a social setting, I might attempt to recover it as I look to anyone around me for some type of validation. Now that I'm aware that this doesn't work, I must actively practice switching my focus from confidence to courage. Why? Because courage is within my immediate control, while confidence is built over time. With courage, my only goal is to face my fear and move through it. I don't need to look too far ahead and attach myself to what is on the other end. Once I've taken that step, I can celebrate in the success of my mission, and I know that it's fully in my control, every time. I can surrender to the process and release my attachment to the outcome I'd originally hoped for, which is a positive reaction from the crowd. (A crowd could be one person or one million people.) Courage saves me from paralysis and allows me to take a step forward, testing myself in new situations. As I experience something new, my fear of the unknown dissipates. Each act of courage contributes to building another solid block of confidence.

The second step is that I must focus on giving rather than getting. When I do this, I naturally release my attachment to the outcome and, paradoxically, I'm much more likely to achieve it. Paul and I became good friends after that lunch, and we began meeting regularly to talk about life with the same depth as we did the first time. During another lunch meeting, he shared his daily mantra with me: "Every day when I wake up, I actively try to think about how I can love everyone I meet more today than I did yesterday." He wasn't describing love from a romantic perspective. That word used to make me cringe in discomfort, perhaps because I didn't know how to separate romantic love from pure love. But when Paul shared this mantra, I knew what he meant.

Love is giving of yourself for the other person's sake, with no intention of personal benefit. It is the release of any judgment. Because Paul challenged himself each day to find ways to do that, he stumbled upon the secret to a happy and effective life. His focus in his performances is to make people feel good. Not only did this give meaning to his musical talent (a "why" for what he does), but it changed his aim away from *getting* something. He certainly still wants to benefit from the fruits of his labor, but that's not his primary focus. Paul has also realized that music isn't his only tool. He can make people feel good outside of his performances as well, by creating safe environments where everyone feels seen and everyone feels equal. If you meet him, you will never feel like a stranger. You won't be intimidated to say hello, and you might even feel compelled to share things with him that will surprise you. You will always feel safe to be you. The real you.

When we focus on creating this space for others, we realize our importance in the world, and we stop focusing on trying to figure out where we fit in. The only way to accomplish this is to be authentic, and this might uncover some things we need to personally work on, but that sparks the journey of our personal growth. It works from the inside out. Our focus on giving saves us from fear of judgment because we've steered our attention away from receiving anything. Judgment, after all, is a form of receiving. It's just the kind we don't want. Stop focusing on what you're going to *get*, and you'll be much more likely to receive great things.

NO ATTACHMENTS

Now, when I'm on a sales call, speaking to a group, or playing music at a campfire, I understand that I must shift my aim toward giving to the other person. Whether I want to educate them or entertain them, it's for *their* benefit. The best way to accomplish this is to give of myself, to take a leap of faith in releasing my inhibitions, and to share what I can, without concern of how it is received. I might still mess up, but it won't paralyze me. Instead of the crowd feeling sorry for me, it may even endear them to me, as they'll see a touch of my humanity. They'll be able to more easily relate, appreciating that even on a high, others are imperfect and vulnerable too. This is how we relate and find inspiration in others. We watch them expose themselves and overcome the same fears, insecurities, and challenges that we fear. When we do this for ourselves, we give light to others, demonstrating what is possible for them.

If the first step is to honestly acknowledge my emotions, and the second is to focus on giving rather than getting, then the third step is to remind myself never to forget the second step. As we become more comfortable in situations, we require less courageous energy than we did in our previous attempts. We start to trust the process and, as our confidence builds, we pay less attention to nervous energy. If we need it at all, courage isn't as crucial a tool as once was required. Sometimes, we feel so confident that we forget to open up. We become less relatable and, consequently, we're less effective in touching others. Anytime I'm required to share, even for something as simple as being called upon in a meeting to communicate a thought, it serves me well to prime myself in advance—to mentally prepare by asking how I can really contribute to the others in my company. If this is the case, I never have to worry about mental blocks because both my mind and heart are open; thus, my creative energy can be released.

MENTAL PREPARATION

Before a sales call, meeting, party, or any situation where you might feel discomfort, imagine the circumstances, and don't make them easy. Picture yourself being who you want to be in each situation. For example, if you're feeling anxious en route, picture yourself being relaxed (if that's what you're after). Enact that in your mind, and if you have trouble doing so, go back to a time where you were in that state. Remembering how it felt is the best way to summon the feeling now. If you're afraid of being stumped when asked a question, picture yourself handling it with grace, poise, and confidence. It helps if you can think back to a time where you did this well, because it allows you to use the version of yourself that you've already experienced as an avatar for your upcoming experience. If you've never actually done it before, and you don't know how that's supposed to look and feel, think of someone you've witnessed doing it. Others who have provided me with a service inspire this in me all the time. I've developed my persona by inspiration from watching admired professionals handle things in a way I would love to replicate. I imagine being inside their minds, experiencing how that confidence would feel and what the audience's response toward them looks like through their eyes.

It seems contradictory that in one breath I suggest you stop focusing so much on yourself, and in the next breath, I tell you to focus on things within yourself. Summon courage? That's looking within. Think of yourself in your future situation? That's self-focus. Think of how you're going to act? More self-focus. *What the fuck, Amyotte? Make up your mind!* The truth is that you can never get away from yourself, and you shouldn't try. There's a healthy way to self-focus and an unhealthy way. Whenever you're unsure, and you need your own answer, go back to what should be your favorite question: Does it serve me?

CHAPTER 15

HEALTHY SELF-FOCUS

When I'm in a sales meeting and I don't get the client, or if I lose a client I already had, it's easy to dismiss and blame the situation or even the client for not "getting it." And that very well may be the case, because business is complex, and people are even more complex. We don't know what we don't know, and some mystic force may just be pulling them away. There are a lot of irrational people out there who don't work with reason. If I don't want to feel bad, I can conclude that the situation wasn't meant to be. I can also recognize that I don't know what is going on in that person's life. Maybe he's stressed and not thinking straight. Though that might be true, what's more productive, before I bring that thought to a close, is to contemplate how I could better navigate the situation to help that person. If I'm in business, surely I'll run into another complex situation. I'll run into another client who has personal challenges that cloud his ability to see what he should. If my goal is to be effective in my craft, then I have to be open to the idea that I can adjust my own approach to better communicate with each specific person.

Healthy self-focus should be a creative state, not a destructive one. This doesn't mean that we don't experience times when we feel bad knowing we could have done better in a situation. This certainly shouldn't be avoided, because if we ignore those times, we rob ourselves of the creativity that follows our initial pain. When we identify areas where we can improve, we can find ways to develop better behavior that ultimately creates a better life. But if we ignore it, in an attempt to protect the little confidence we already have, we block our vision for the possibility of a better us, and thus a better life.

If I made the attempt to see the situation through their lens instead of mine, what would I see? What would I feel? And then, what would help me to better navigate the situation? Perhaps I might see that I didn't communicate enough. Or perhaps, because my client isn't confident, he was looking to draw from *my* confidence, and he saw a crack in it. If I, the professional, wasn't confident enough in my advice, how could he be? Now, if this were true, would the breakdown in trust really be his fault or mine? Perhaps I might notice that my client is always perfectly dressed, his car is perfectly clean, and he's always perfectly on time, which means he values order. Perhaps he noticed my dirty shoes or that I was five minutes late for an appointment. Because it's human nature to assume that how we do *something* is how we do *everything*, perhaps he didn't think that I take enough care in my work as a result. I may agree or disagree with that view, but commiserating about how he should think differently doesn't solve the problem. I'd be better served to get my shit in order for the next time we meet, because I know that clean shoes and showing up on time has never jeopardized my chance of a sale.

Of course, those would all be assumptions. Had I addressed those items, would my results have changed? Unless I could reverse time, I would never know. Either way, I've found areas to work on for the next situation. As I eliminate potential reasons for failing my next mission, I can become more competent and more confident in my craft. All of this self-focus allowed me to create the possibility of becoming more effective, which means that I might create better results. It's still painful to look in the mirror and realize that the image I have of myself isn't in line with the image my client had of me, but it's productive. If I take the twenty-thousand-foot view, I'll gladly accept short-term pain and trade it for long-term gain. With that, I can be grateful for an experience that at first seemed like a loss but, in reality, was the very experience I needed to win bigger in the future.

INSIDE OUT

When we suffer from failure, we're often not willing to look within because it hurts. So we tend to look to the external to justify our failure. This is the time to self-focus, but we have to do it with care and compassion for ourselves, just as we would for our children, best friend, or spouse, because it's not about beating ourselves up over something we could have done better. It's not about creating regret for something we can't change. It's about reclaiming our personal power. We do this by honoring a negative situation and transforming it into a positive one. When we can do this, we'll never curse our failures again. At least, not once we come out of the other side of the work that follows our self-reflection.

Positive self-focus is when we look from the inside out. We look internally at how we affect our world. Then, once we find the right version of ourselves that can correct what is needed, we project it externally. Negative self-focus is when we look from the outside in. We make assumptions about what the outside world sees in us, and then we look within, which triggers us to project that negative thought we imagined. With this approach, we lose the creative power to project what we want, and instead, we bring our fear—the very thing we're trying to avoid—to life. If we're fixated on our audience's thoughts, hoping that their energy will help us out, we become more vulnerable to thoughts of inadequacy when the right energy isn't happening for us. With this, we shrink back, and our voices weaken. We might even become so paralyzed in the moment that we forget what we want to say. We close the floodgates of inspired, free-flowing thought, and we certainly don't share the best version of ourselves. It's impossible to give of ourselves when we're having an out-of-body experience, with our thoughts fixated on what others are seeing of us in this long, awkward moment.

Improper self-focus doesn't just backfire on us in a presentation. It negates our objectives in conflict with other people. It holds us back in our businesses and careers. It hinders the development of our children, and it keeps us from growing rich relationships with friends, family, and loved ones. When our unconscious objective is personal benefit, we make different choices. It's not always malicious, and it's not always obvious. Good, caring people are just as susceptible to falling into this trap. A caring mother whose children are her world might coddle them, keeping them from growing and becoming independent, as they aren't given the opportunity to stumble and learn to overcome adversity without her help. Her intentions are well-meaning, as she aims to protect them, but if she's overprotecting, is that really for their security, or is it for her own? If she isn't willing to deal with her own fears and insecurities, her children will become the victims of her unwillingness to reconsider what is truly best for her children.

A person whose main objective with friends is to lean on them in solving their own problems might appreciate the love and care that is shared with them, but is it reciprocal? If their interest in virtually all interactions is themselves, it eventually wears on their friends. Even the most loyal and giving friends will, in due course, resent the imbalance of give and take in their relationship. (If this might be you, try calling your friend and asking how they're doing. Be genuine. Make your conversation about them for the entire call, without ever bringing it back to you. Watch your relationship grow, as you'll both benefit from the change in focus.)

A business that offers a great product or service might also have all the right systems in place and plenty of talent, but if it forgets that the purpose of its existence is to serve its customer, that business will eventually flounder. If the business's primary goal is self-advancement or profit for its shareholders, they will make shortsighted decisions, and the customers will feel it. No matter how good the business is now, when the economy shifts or consumer behavior evolves, it won't know how to pivot, as it'll be blinded by its own need for immediate self-advancement.

An outside-in perspective spawns decisions that feel like they benefit us in the present, but they often hurt others along the way and ultimately impair our long-term objectives. We throw ourselves on a perpetual treadmill, constantly chasing our dreams and desires, but no matter what we achieve, we never fill that empty area inside of us and we feel alone in our mission. We buy into the story that personal gain must sometimes come at the cost of others' well-being, *or* we blind ourselves from that responsibility altogether because it's too painful to accept the truth of our role in their demise.

INTEGRATING INTERESTS

When our goals aren't inclusive, it's no wonder we feel alone. We're literally separating ourselves from humanity in our quest for self-advancement. To create true success, integration is the proper recipe. When we focus on the service of others, they feel it and reciprocate. While it's true that some people are purely takers, the sum total of humans is better than that; therefore, it's still a winning strategy. We still must protect ourselves from being taken advantage of, so you must remind yourself that *you* are also one of the people you serve. You should protect yourself the same way you would protect your friends and your loved ones. Once you've set your standards for how you want to be treated, you'll know your boundaries when it comes to the service of others. We get what we tolerate, and unless we're aware of what that standard is, we can fall victim to acts of careless takers. Draw a line in the sand, and don't let anyone cross it. When you do this, you can now set your sights back to servicing others and away from protecting yourself. If others try to cross the line you've drawn, stand your ground. With this, you're training them to stay within their boundaries. Most people don't try to cross boundaries maliciously. They have egos too, and if they haven't yet learned the secret to integrating their success with yours, crossing your boundaries is often an unconscious act. Have compassion for this, and you won't be so offended by the takers. You might even influence them to awaken and change their behavior, not just toward you, but toward others as well.

When you integrate another's best interest with your own, they can feel it, and they reciprocate. Together, you create an environment of safety. When we feel safe, we allow our best selves to deliver and thus further develop our best gifts. It's difficult to do this in self-protection mode. We wear an armor that restricts us from moving freely, as it weighs us down. When we're thinking about protecting ourselves, we aren't thinking about the wonderful possibilities of the future. We're stuck thinking about not being attacked.

COMPARISON

How do you feel when you compare yourself to others? If you think through a few scenarios, you might respond with, "It depends." And you would be right. One scenario might raise you up, while another might tear you down. Imagine a teacher grades a test on a curve, and you score 40 percent, but the class average is 20 percent. There's solace in still being at the top of your class despite a terrible score.

When I started in real estate, if I sold three homes in a single month, I should have been proud of a great sales month. But if I compared myself to a top producer who'd been in the business for twenty years and finished with thirty sales that month, should I have been less proud? What if I compared myself to another veteran agent who'd been in the business for twenty-five years but only sold two homes that month? Should that have made me feel good? If it did, should the veteran agent then have felt bad? I guess it would depend on the story we each told ourselves.

Imagine you're a newer golfer, or you only play on occasion. When you go out with your friends who golf five rounds per week, take lessons, and adore the sport, do you compare your play to theirs? When you don't play as well as them, would you conclude that you suck, and golf isn't the sport for you? Comparison is a useful tool if you view it through a compassionate lens. If you're like me and tend to get down on yourself for not being as good as others in your company, it would serve you well to shift your thoughts away from self-pity and toward curiosity. Be curious as to how your friends are playing well or how the top real estate agent is able to sell ten times as many homes as you are. Take into account all the factors that come into play. How much time have they spent in practice? What systems have they developed? Who have they talked to or learned from? How do they think? What is their approach? What challenges did they need to overcome, and which do they continue to work on? If you ask with genuine curiosity, you'll be amazed at how much they might be willing to share and how much you can learn. Then, the next questions you should ask yourself are: If you truly want better results, are you capable of investing in all the same approaches they did? Can you put in more time? Is it possible to engage the help of others? Is it possible to work on developing your own systems? If you ignore the possibilities of your own capability, you're not exactly playing a fair comparison game. So the real question to ask is this: Do I want it as much as they do?

When you admire someone for their tremendous accomplishments, do you put them on a pedestal? It's hard to speak with confidence when you think this person knows everything you do and more. You build up stories in your mind about their competence, and if you subconsciously put them at the top of your internal hierarchy, you place yourself lower as a consequence. Your physiology weakens, and the other person feels it. They only take you as seriously as you take yourself, and you diminish your own power. Confident and competent people enjoy the company of competent and confident people. They don't care if you know less or are capable of less. They just care that your thirst for growth matches theirs. Confident people want to be inspired by others, and they appreciate any place you currently sit within your journey. You can still admire their traits and accomplishments without assuming hierarchies. Their accomplishments don't negate yours, because you aren't competing.

This is how a rookie salesperson can still win a sale with an ultra-successful client. This is how a young, driven person can win the time and attention of a veteran they admire. It's how a regular Joe can become friends with someone of stature. No truly confident person wants to be put on a pedestal, because it deprives them of their humanity. It does this in exact proportion in the opposite way when we put ourselves on a pedestal toward another whom we deem lesser based on a judgment we've made. Perhaps they've made a mistake that we haven't, or they continuously struggle with something that comes easy to us. Either way, when we create false hierarchies of human value, we ignore empathy for the battles of others and dehumanize our interactions with them.

COMPASSION

If the previous section made sense to you, you can now bring compassion to those who create hierarchies for us. If they put others down to build themselves up, perhaps we can instead look to them with empathy and realize that they do this because they lack confidence themselves. A few words of encouragement might give them what they're after, and in time, it might help them see a different strategy of their own. This act blocks them from building the social construct they attempt in an effort to enhance their own confidence and security. We never have to feel inferior as a result of someone else's attempt to build their social hierarchy. Recognize that we're all on the same playing field, we're all fighting our own battle within our own unique journey, and we each have different strengths and weaknesses. This is the paradigm that allows us to be inspired by others rather than discouraged. We learn from them rather than feeling threatened. We dream bigger as a substitute to playing defense. We grow excited about a brighter future, and we come to not just believe, but to *understand* that it's actually possible.

CHAPTER 16

SELF-SABOTAGE

———

It was a typical cold and snowy winter, as we could expect in Northern Alberta. I had just completed the highest-producing year I'd ever had selling real estate, and that momentum carried us into 2014 with full steam. Avarey and I were almost finished renovating our home in the area where all my wealthy friends from high school had lived. I was in the best physical shape I'd ever been in, and I could take my family on amazing vacations that I had only dreamed of as a kid. I had the respect of people that I never thought possible, and my personal network was expanding. As far as I was concerned, I had made it, and I wasn't even thirty yet. Not bad for a kid who moved away from home in the ninth grade and who never thought he would amount to anything. I wasn't exactly rich, but I was fortunate. Save for the business challenges, which I was accustomed to working through, nothing was really going wrong. I wasn't used to that.

Avarey and I had booked a weekend ski trip in the mountains. We were to make the four-hour drive to the famous ski town of Banff, Alberta, and meet two other couples there. At the time, I was in conversation with the Porsche dealer to upgrade my car. I had a great relationship with the staff, and they graciously offered to lend me the car that I was thinking of purchasing to take on our trip. What a treat! I was elated to drive this car through the mountain roads.

When we made it to Banff, our friends were already there waiting for us. Before we even unloaded our luggage, I offered to take my friend Marc for a quick drive. When you're with another car enthusiast, it's a given that you show them what the car is capable of, so I pushed the Sport Plus button and took off. You can't fully appreciate a Porsche until you take it around tight corners, as that is where it truly shines. They handle the roads like nothing else.

I took the car around an overpass at full throttle, no hesitation or even a hint of letting off the gas. It's not the proper way to take a corner, even for experienced race car drivers. But on that day, I felt that I should test my limits, as well as the car's. Besides, the shock factor for my friend in the passenger seat would make it all worth it. The traction control system of a Porsche works incredibly well. It can mask driver mistakes and make us feel like we're better drivers than we really are. Until it doesn't.

The side of the overpass had gravel on it. My back tires were barely holding the road, and once they caught the gravel, I completely lost control. The car was thrown off the road, down into the snow-covered ditch, and into a swale, and shot back up to catch a lip before the highway. We soared into the air, cleared the shoulder, then, still in the air, flew over the first lane of the main highway. The tires finally hit the pavement once we were well into the second lane. I pumped the brakes as fast and as hard as I could while manually gearing down, but it wasn't enough to keep us from crossing into the next ditch. I continued to pump the brakes, but the snow-covered grass was unforgiving, and our momentum continued until the car smashed head-on into a median and stopped dead in its tracks. The front of the car tilted forward as the back end bounced up a few feet in the air before it made its final stop.

Once the airbags softened, I looked over at Marc to make sure he was okay. He was good. So was I, though I immediately felt remorse. My first thought was that I knew I could have made that corner at the same speed. I wanted to do it again. Then a terrible guilt came over me. I felt ashamed for letting down the staff at the dealership, who had entrusted me to respect their $150,000 vehicle. Having my insurance company buy it wasn't exactly how they planned to sell me that car.

Two hours later, after the police report was filed and the totaled car was hauled away, we had drinks and laughed it off. I went skiing the next day like nothing had ever happened. My wife and friends were baffled at how I was handling the shock of the crash. As much as it seemed like nothing had happened to me on the outside, though, something was bubbling on the inside. It bothered me that the crash didn't bother me. It bothered me that my very first thought was, *I want to do that again. I know I'm a better driver than that.* I had no regard for how lucky we were that no cars were crossing that busy highway at the moment we flew across it at triple-digit speeds. Seconds sooner and lives may have been lost—but I wasn't thinking of that. I was thinking of how I could just "be better" behind the steering wheel.

OVERWHELM

Weeks passed, and I kept replaying the crash in my mind. I went about my life as if everything was normal, but something wasn't right. One Friday, I met one of my best friends at a restaurant for lunch. With no agenda, when I sat down, he asked me how I was doing. I wasn't expecting it, but the simple question gave me permission to let go, and I completely broke down. Tears streamed down my face uncontrollably, and I sat silently crying, with Ron simply watching and trying to figure me out. I couldn't gather myself to say even one word.

I didn't even know it was coming. It's as if I had been compressing all the pressures of life, and they all shot out at once. When I could finally muster a few words, all I could say was, "I'm tired of being the strong one. I can't do it anymore." I was depended on by many people for many different reasons. Because I cared, I took on everyone's stresses and problems and made them my own. But I'd always enjoyed that. It made me feel important because I could make a difference. I did this for my staff, my friends, my kids, my clients, and even my dogs. I was overwhelmed with a sense of responsibility. It suddenly felt like an obligation to drive business so I could pay the bills, so my sales staff could put food on their tables, so everyone could be happy, and so I could continue to be liked and respected by everyone.

Once you've created this image of who you are or who you think other people think you are, you feel this pressure to uphold that, even when you can't. I had grown a reputation for being the one who had it all together, who made all the right choices, and who could handle anything that came my way. Only I couldn't be that person anymore. At least not at that moment.

That year, it was as if I was looking for something that was wrong in my life. I decided that I wasn't happy in my marriage, as I spoke about in previous chapters. This is what led up to it. Shaking up my marriage led to incredibly rocky times. All the certainty of who I was and where I was headed in life was gone. When I had the realization that the problems were entirely my own, I was able to dissect my behavior.

WHEN FEAR NO LONGER SERVES YOU

I came from a place in my youth where I truly didn't believe I would amount to anything, and I think most people in my life wouldn't have been surprised if that was how it unfolded. My behavior as a teenager left no clues that I was headed along the right path. When I started working in real estate, my initial drive to learn, and my ability to grind away for ninety hours each and every week, was stimulated almost exclusively by fear. I was scared of not making it. I was afraid of not having enough money to pay my bills. I was worried I wouldn't be respected—by others in the industry, by my clients, by anyone I knew.

Fear served me well, but when the struggles I was accustomed to fighting went away, so did the fear. I didn't know what could keep me motivated. I was addicted to struggling, so when I ran out of the struggles I had, I fabricated more. I wasn't fully aware of this at the time, but subconsciously, I didn't feel worthy or deserving of the life that I had dreamed of in my youth. When I had made it, I didn't know how to handle a peaceful life. While sometimes I worked to build something good into something better, at other times I sabotaged those great things in an effort to reproduce the excitement and satisfaction of going through them again.

I didn't want to lose my inner drive and motivation, so I looked for a new challenge. I hated the thought of becoming complacent, but I also didn't want to let go of all the great things I already had. How could I achieve both? My inner drive was starting to drain me. My motivation couldn't continue to be about what I might lose or what was missing in my life. I knew that fear could no longer fuel me, but what was the antidote?

The answer I discovered was *love*. I had to change my mindset and consider what I could contribute. I had to focus on what could be rather than what was not. It was a pull toward something that I knew I could give to the world rather than a push from the anxiety of being swept up by the things I didn't want in life.

PEACE OF MIND

I thought that success was something to pursue. But what is success? As the great speaker Jim Rohn once said, "Success is something that we attract by who we become." I now realize that, in its purest form, success is peace of mind. It is the legitimate effort of living every moment of life in line with our true values. That doesn't mean that we do this without fail, but it is a direction. Like a compass, we check in with ourselves and adjust the course when we've drifted off.

When I began to sabotage my life, I didn't need to look any further than assessing my values. There is an inner torment in times of pain and, as difficult as it is to think clearly in the midst of chaos, I realized that the pain wasn't rooted in the events that were happening to me. The pain was a reaction to violating the principles that mattered to me, the way in which I lived my life, and how I affected the world around me. It steered me back to the true me that I had set out to become.

This is the importance of being clear on our values. Though my subconscious didn't believe that I deserved the life I had built for myself, it still believed that, with each choice I faced, I should make the one that complements my values rather than violates them. When you give to the universe with good intentions, it can't help but eventually give you something in return. In light of this, how can *any one* person ever think that they deserve anything less than another? The old cliché that "we are all created equal" has been overused to the point where we don't actually believe it. The truth is that we are all created. Period. And we all create. Period. Much of what we create is by choice. When we choose to create out of love—with the intention of contributing to other people, to our planet, to anything outside of ourselves—the universe doesn't discern which neighborhood we're born in, who we know, who our parents are, or what our grades were in school. Reciprocity has no judgment. It simply gives back to those who give.

In order to give out of love, we must love ourselves, because it's too difficult to give something we don't have. Paradoxically, the best way to receive love is to give it without anticipating it coming back to us. I believe that every one of us is ultimately trying to find acceptance in this world. To achieve that, we first have to accept both ourselves and others. When we truly surrender to who we are, clarity ensues, and the universe gives us exactly what we're looking for.

CHAPTER 17

CHANGING PERSPECTIVES

———

My self-sabotage was a painful one. I created chaos and uncertainty that hadn't previously existed. In a crazy way, it was one of the most important things I had ever done. It challenged me to look deep within myself and to understand why I behaved the way I did. When I understood my deep-rooted beliefs, I could finally challenge them. *Does this belief serve me? Where does it come from? Is it valid?*

Very few things in life are absolute. People give opinions as if they are the only truth. An opinion is simply a perspective filtered through the lens of that person's past experiences. This said, if I wipe away my own past experiences and look through the lens of someone in a position that I would prefer to be in, what would I see differently? Can I adapt that as well? If their view has served them, and if it helps to reach a similar goal to one that I'm after, it's probably a perspective worth trying to adapt myself.

I am not less deserving than the most fortunate person on Earth. I am also not more deserving than the most unfortunate person on Earth. We are all born from different places, and we're dealt different hands. We perceive some to be more fortunate than others, and there is no doubt that some must endure more pain that's out of their control, while others appear to have everything handed to them. Those of us who are born in developed countries almost automatically have our basic human needs met the moment we enter this world. We're free to work the jobs we want, open the businesses we want, live where we want, and love whom we want—if we just choose to go after those things. Though we often struggle to see it, we have equal opportunity, and each of us is deserving of exactly what we believe we are. It is easier to see opportunities in others because we're removed from the story—the one we tell ourselves about why we're different. It's easier to see the potential in others and to let go of any excuses around why they aren't deserving of success. It's harder to see it in ourselves, because when we let go of our excuses, we have no more excuses, and the only thing left is to get to work.

I didn't think I deserved to be free of financial struggle, and it was because that was how I had lived my entire childhood. I didn't think I was deserving of a great marriage because I hadn't witnessed one growing up. Any experience of the opposite seemed like I was just there for a short visit, and I would eventually have to go back to the comfort of my unhappiness. I didn't believe that I was deserving or capable of writing a book, because I didn't know any "real" writers. To me, authors were mystical people who lived far away, who came from something I didn't, and therefore could do something that I couldn't. Anytime I would go after a dream of something better, once I surpassed my expectation, I would subconsciously steer myself back to what was comfortable.

SHAPING WHO YOU ARE

When you meet and surround yourself with people who are achieving things that you admire, it slowly breaks down the barriers. The better you get to know them, the more you realize they, too, have weaknesses—even some that you don't have. They, too, have insecurities, but the difference is that they still press on. And slowly, with time, they start to believe in themselves. It's not linear. It is a broken path of ups, downs, rights, lefts, and backwards, but they press on, with the ultimate direction being forward. It is a daily battle, but we must never lose sight of our aim. Every day that we fight back the urge to retreat to what is comfortable, every day that we question the beliefs that do not serve our purpose, we grow ourselves out of them, and our self-assurance develops within us as we move forward.

It is our tendency to believe that our past shapes our future.

Why? Because it does if we allow it to. Your past experiences are like ninjas sneaking into your subconscious. Each contributes to your personal narrative by creating explanations for how the world works. Those cultivated beliefs affect the choices that you make in the present day, which ultimately create your life tomorrow. With this knowledge, we can question our beliefs and bring awareness to the choices we're making each day. The real truth is that today's actions determine tomorrow's reality. We can't change our past, but we can choose our actions in the present. As we build consistency in the actions we take, we create a brighter future. Then, one day, we'll look back and realize that our reality looks different. Over time, our inner narrative evolves, and we begin to believe in different possibilities. But we can't let go of that aim!

Here's the crazy part. In this context, we aren't just creating our future lives. We are purely creating ourselves. There are certainly strong genetic predispositions that never go away, but as we change our thoughts, we rewire our ways of thinking, which ultimately shape who we become. Performing a specific physical activity with consistency will transform your body. The same person who performs gymnastics every day can then quit and begin to body build, and his body will change into something different. Alternatively, he can stop being physical altogether, and his body will change into something different, yet again. Then, maybe he will take up long-distance running and look different still. The same person on four different paths will create four completely different bodies. Just as our bodies adapt to what it is called for, so do our minds. This is why it's so important to be aware of what we're taking in. From the thoughts we have in our own head to the conversations we have with others, from the television shows we watch to the books we read, every thought we have contributes to shaping who we are. Choose your thoughts wisely.

DIG DEEPER

My saving grace in life was getting around people who inspire me and finding a way to truly get to know them. When people let us in and allow us to see who they really are, they permit us to see that they are flawed, just as we are. In some circumstances, this causes us disappointment. Each of us puts certain people on a pedestal. We want to believe that they have a greatness that the rest of us don't, as that would justify their unique achievements. Have you ever thought to yourself about someone, *I don't know how he is so successful. He's not that smart!* or *She's a terrible communicator!* or that someone lacks whatever quality you believe is necessary for achievement? Then, instead of being curious, you chalk it up to luck. Rather than figuring out how they work around their weakness, you move on, letting yourself off the hook for your lack of accomplishment.

If we were to engage in curiosity and really wanted to know that person deeply, really get to know their story, their insecurities, and their stumbling blocks, we would find that, in most circumstances, those people were willing to dig deeper, fight harder and longer, and therefore develop those special qualities that we saw in the first place. The flaws we see are the remnants of the person he began as, or the scars left behind from his battle of becoming who he is. That person is still on his journey of development and always will be. It's never over. We're constantly working on ourselves, and the more we keep pushing to do so, the more confident we become. With more confidence, we eventually attract better results to our lives.

Seeing that others have achieved greatness despite their flaws exposes us. It exposes that we are simply making excuses for not having—or at least not going for—what we truly want in life. That's why we're filled with disappointment. It's also why some people hesitate to be real with others. They're afraid of the judgment.

The celebrity who doesn't seem approachable to her fans is that way because too many of us fail to see the humanity in her. We see her as something we are not and set our expectations of her higher than the expectations we place on ourselves. We say things like "She gets paid millions of dollars. She can handle it." But does getting paid more money mean that she trades in her human flaws? Those expectations are another form of putting others on a pedestal. Having different expectations of people we've never met than the ones we would have of our sons, daughters, and friends only means that we stopped trying to relate. We failed to acknowledge their humanity and to feel what they feel. We can't look past what they have externally. We assume that the trade they must accept is to put up with the worst sides of the "rest of us." But where is our own personal responsibility?

PEDESTALS

What if we put ourselves on the same pedestal as those we look up to? What if we put the blood, sweat, tears, and determination into our goals that we know they did for theirs? What if we held ourselves to the same standard of how to treat others all the time? My bet is this:

1. We would have more respect and admiration for high achievers.
2. We would have more empathy for others' challenges.
3. We would believe in ourselves more. We would achieve more, and just maybe, we would begin to realize that we're equally deserving of more.

The more we reach, the more we expose our vulnerabilities. Then we realize that we're all the same. We all have things that we love to do and things that we don't like doing. When we go for big things that we love, it is often necessary to do things that we don't love. When we're pushed to our breaking point, it's hard to predict how we're going to react. I think I know myself so well until I put myself in a situation foreign to me, then I get to know an entirely different facet of myself that I didn't know existed. (This is a great reason to be comfortable with continuous discomfort.)

In light of this, each one of us is capable of so much more than we know. But we'll never know unless we push ourselves to go after those little thoughts of *What if?* or *What about?* or *I Wonder* or *I Bet.* There's no question that when you go for bigger things, you'll be uncomfortable and you'll question whether it's worth the hassle. When we're in the midst of the storm, it's hard to see, but nothing lasts forever. When things are good, just wait. And when things are bad, just wait. Once we're out of the shit, we realize it's always worth it, even if we failed. I believe that the point of life is very simple. It is to experience *life*, and to consciously become. The more we push ourselves to develop, the more we experience. When every day feels like Groundhog Day, and you ask yourself why you're not happy, that is your soul telling you to step out of your comfort zone. It may not necessarily require a massive change, but that unsettled feeling means it's time for something new. We all have an innate desire to grow in some capacity, and the only thing holding us back from doing so is ourselves.

It is never quite certain exactly how we'll grow. We don't know precisely who we'll end up becoming on the other end, but we can set the direction by our goals, habits, and dreams. We just can't attach ourselves too firmly to the outcome. When you start to steer yourself back in the direction of your past, take a break. Take a twenty-thousand-foot view and be clear on what you're doing and why. *Do not fear success.* It is for everyone, not just the "others."

CHAPTER 18

EXCELLENCE

Taking massive action to revolutionize our lives sounds like a winning strategy. We're inspired to do so as we read a great book, watch a great movie, or perhaps attend a powerful conference that leaves us feeling like we've been given the roadmap to achieve all our dreams. Now we're ready to take on the world with a whole new attitude. But as days pass, *real life* sets in. We might try too hard, too fast, and then we're slowly humbled. We might realize the life we imagined while living in the novelty of new information isn't ours. Or a new life begins to feel out of reach, as we simply don't know *what* to work on to make the dream a reality. The emotions that came from that source of inspiration fade, and it feels like we were stuck in an unrealistic dream state that we've finally awakened from. *What the fuck was I thinking?* Our old programming sets in, and we either give up and settle back into the old us, *or* we scramble to find more inspiration to keep ourselves going. If we want to get that feeling back, we might look for new books, new videos, or new education, and we might stumble upon something novel that sparks the same excitement. Then it wears off again, and we find more material. Before we know it, we become professional consumers of motivation. It's like a drug that keeps us feeling good. We often realize that, though it supplies us with our daily dopamine dump and makes us feel like we're doing something productive, if we're honest with ourselves, the only action we're really taking is consuming better material. Eventually, we might decide that it's all bullshit, as we feel cheated when we realize that nothing has changed.

There is nothing wrong with consuming great material. It's far healthier than consuming negative media coverage and unproductive social media posts. There is a place for it, and it's genuinely important, as it helps us reshape our views about how the world works. Don't stop! However, if we rely solely on this external motivation to keep us going, it will eventually fail us, and we'll fail ourselves as a result.

YOUR GREATEST SOURCE OF INSPIRATION

What happens when you don't feel like you have a dream to work toward? What happens when you're tired, or numb, or you simply feel satisfied with it all? First, it's important to note that none of those feelings are permanent. It's worth stepping back and appreciating your current state.

But don't get fooled into thinking that this is just *who you are*. Don't fool yourself into thinking that you just simply aren't a "go-getter" or you aren't self-motivated. That's bullshit. It simply means you haven't discovered how to tap into your greatest source of inspiration—the one you can always count on. And what would that be? Your greatest source of inspiration is *you*.

Inspiration is an energy. It is a momentum we create by practicing one simple virtue. It's not about practicing massive feats and conquering the world. That might come as an aftereffect, one that appears monumental from the outside looking in, but that which we see over time is simply a projection of the collection of our daily practice in the virtue of *excellence*. Excellence affords us the opportunity to progress each and every day, no matter how we feel. In fact, excellence is easier to identify when we're completely unmotivated, uninspired, numb, and satisfied. Why? Because excellence is simply doing more than what we feel like doing. And what better opportunity to practice excellence than when we don't feel like doing anything? When we do more than we feel like and we push ourselves a little farther than we think we can go, we initiate momentum. Done consistently, we'll surprise ourselves a little more each time. Then, eventually, we develop curiosity. We create wonder for what could be—unattached to the end result—because we realize that the largest part of the enjoyment comes *not* from achieving specific results but from experiencing the process of transformation.

A DESCRIPTION OF EXCELLENCE

Excellence is when you have a million things to do, you're tired, and the last thing you want to get done is your workout, but you go anyway because you committed to it before you were tired. When you're there, excellence is when you think your muscles have nothing left to give at the end of your set, but you dig deep and push through the pain to get an extra two push-ups in.

Excellence is when you're busy, and you have too many files to process, but you double- and triple-check all your work even more than normal, because you want to make sure there are no mistakes and you know that you might have more of them *because* you're tired and have a lot on your plate. What you want to do is the exact opposite, because when you're burned out, it requires triple the effort to get it right, but you do it right anyway. Then you enjoy your rest with the satisfaction of a good day's work.

Excellence is knowing there's a skill you're not proficient enough in that hinders you and your team, preventing you from being more effective, and though you hate it, you work on developing that skill because you know it will bring better results.

Excellence is getting constant feedback that there's part of you that hurts others close to you, so—though it doesn't bother you—you work on channeling that elsewhere and develop a different side of your personality.

Excellence is practicing courage. It is doing the things you're afraid of or uncomfortable doing because you know they will help you grow into the person you want to become.

Excellence is making the phone call you don't want to make. When it's easier to either text, email, or ignore it altogether—because some conversations are just hard, annoying, or uncomfortable—you make the call anyway. You do this because you know that the most difficult conversations are often the most important ones to have.

In essence, excellence is doing the things we don't want to do, because we care more about results than we do about appeasing our own immediate feelings. To act despite our feelings in service of future results is self-mastery. It's also self-love for the future *you*. Because what you do today creates your environment tomorrow. The more your present self does to create a better reality for your future self, the more confidence you gain because you learn to trust yourself in following through on your own commitments. The bond between you and your past self grows, eliminating feelings of doubt and regret. As you gain positive momentum, doing the difficult things in life becomes easier and eventually grows into a habit—something you do naturally without conscious thought. It becomes who you are. Paradoxically, as we do this with consistency, we begin to enjoy the present more and more. We start to love where we are today and become excited about the possibilities we're creating for ourselves tomorrow.

To practice excellence is to *excel*. To excel means to move forward, and in order to move to a better place, we need to be honest with ourselves on *where* we currently are. We need to be honest about our gifts and about the areas that hold us back from creating the success we truly want to achieve. We might already know what those are, *but* we might not. Being honest requires vulnerability. There's no way around that because we accept both the good and the bad. Some of us tend to accept our faults more than our gifts, while others accept their gifts and refuse to acknowledge their faults. Some of us ignore both altogether, keeping ourselves numb from any emotion. This way, we don't have to worry about disappointment. If we're truly after progress, however, we cannot hide from ourselves. The only way your exterior circumstances can change is for *you* to change. All success starts from within. It starts from the inside out.

Excellence doesn't discern at what speed we advance. Acknowledge your progress, regardless of its cadence. Allow yourself to be encouraged and to get excited about your genuine effort. Be proud of inching forward, and be curious about what comes next if you keep going. Do not focus on the gap between where you are and what is perfect.

Ask others ahead of you for feedback. Remember that feedback isn't "make me feel good." It's "make me better," because the aim is the result, which will make you feel good. If you want to feel good in the process, you'll never get the result, because your illusion of your self-image will hold you back from actually being the person who achieves the result.

AIM FOR THE RESULT, LIVE IN THE PROCESS

If practicing excellence begins to feel like a chore, this is a prompt to stop—at least for a moment. Create a space of peace within the chaos of life in order to self-reflect. Forget everything that is overwhelming you in your current situation and remind yourself of what you're after, because if you're fixated on what you don't like today, it means your focus has drifted from what you're really working to accomplish. It's possible that your focus has zoomed in to the minutiae of today's problems, and now everything feels like a nuisance. You can't focus on two things at once. If you've been sucked into the vortex of cursing the pain of today, zoom your perspective out and recalibrate your choices. Your "why" is your compass. It sets the direction of your daily actions. When you shift your focus back to where you want to go, you won't mind the bullshit that comes each day as much. In fact, you might begin to love it, because now you appreciate that it's all a necessary part of the journey that's taking you where you want to go.

When life seems to be dragging you along, change your pace. Run slower or run faster—just don't stop. You might need a rest before you keep going, but you might not. That's up to you to decide. Be real with yourself, as there's no wrong answer. Different people require different advice. Just don't let yourself off the hook too easily. We don't know what we're capable of until we push ourselves into something we've never done. It hurts, but it's a good hurt because this is how we grow. There should be no greater source of inspiration to you than yourself. Surprise yourself by doing a little more than you think you can. Over time, you'll look back and realize the compounding effects of your daily growth, and you'll eventually realize that you're capable of accomplishing anything you really want, *as long as you truly want it.* Only when you make a true decision will you commit to the process of getting there. When the inevitable challenges start to knock you off course, you'll need to remind yourself of that "why" in order to keep moving in the right direction. Otherwise, if you're simply "interested," the pain of the process won't seem worth the trade, and you'll change your mind, moving back toward the frustration of feeling that your dreams are simply that—dreams that will never come true.

Your daily practice of excellence should feel like a pull toward your goals and aspirations, rather than a push because you "have to." Reflect and ensure your dream is the right one. If it is, yet the work still seems too hard, it's not the dream that needs to be adjusted—it's your attitude. Hard is good. Hard means you're doing something worthwhile. If it were easy, it would be done all the time, and you wouldn't be working toward anything extraordinary. It would simply be ordinary. And ordinary is that place where most people live and wish they had more. It's the space where dreams die because, like trees in a forest, if we aren't growing, we are dying. Don't die until you can do it with a smile on your face, knowing that you developed yourself to your very best capability. You owe it to yourself and to the universe that gifted us with this incredible world to discover who you're capable of becoming. The more you become, the more you experience, and the more you experience, the more you appreciate the gift of life. Don't let comfort stand in your way. Comfort is a trap. It's a lie.

CONCLUSION

LIVING OUR BEST LIFE

———

Life is tricky. We love it, but we hate it. Self-confidence is tricky. It's fleeting, and it's compartmental. It's a necessary ingredient to being effective in our lives, and yet being effective is the very thing that builds it. Like the chicken and the egg; we can confuse ourselves as to which comes first. It serves us well to have it, but its absence can serve us just as well, *if* we know how to handle that. The process of building confidence is what makes life worth living. We discover ourselves, we discover others, and we discover the world, experiencing more of life and appreciating the multitude of facets within it. After all, isn't the point of life to experience life? Then to experience and discover ourselves within it?

As we choose our path and attempt to find our place in

the world, we realize our personal power in our ability to create both. However, when we do this without conscious intention, we might end up in a place we don't want to be. Then we feel lost and confused as we try to make sense of something beyond our comprehension. For this reason, there are few things more important than the practice of self-reflection—spending uninterrupted time with ourselves to develop clarity in the things that really matter to us. When we know what matters, we develop our aim. When we have an aim, we have a purpose—a reason to continue, to be excited about life, and not to quit when we experience the inevitable blows that cause us to question it all.

When that reason is rooted in our contribution to something bigger than ourselves—to what we can give to the world rather than what we can get—we then look deep within to uncover the characteristics we want to develop, free from fear and self-preservation. We realize the honor in letting go of who we are in order to become who we must become, because we know this is how we'll get to where we want to go. It comes with pain, but we embrace it, knowing that it's a necessary part of the journey. Challenge is the resistance that strengthens our values and characteristics. With that, we activate the courage to move *through* our fears, the discipline to take consistent action, and the integrity to follow through to the end, keeping us on course when life attempts to throw us in a new direction. We welcome the test of our commitments because we know they are precisely what strengthens us.

The deeper we follow this path, the stronger we build the bond of trust within ourselves. We accept responsibility for our lives and become the very source of our own inspiration. And it's not just for us, as we shine a light for others, inspiring them and influencing them to do the same. We no longer seek validation from the world, because we're secure in ourselves. We know what we stand for and why we stand for it. We know what we're capable of, despite its degree of difficulty. We can go to bed at night knowing that no matter what life throws at us, we'll figure it out.

This is living our best life. It no longer matters how others are living theirs because we know that we're each on our own unique journey. Sometimes we cross paths, and we can feel grateful for that. If someone achieves something we haven't, we can allow ourselves to be inspired by them, to respond with curiosity, and to build more excitement for life and what we can make of it. Because we put no one on a pedestal and no one in a hole, we realize that each of us is equally as deserving as the next. We're all dealt a different hand, but that's okay because we each have a unique vision of the good life.

Success is defined differently by everyone. My definition is simply to develop along the right path. It is the conscious becoming of who we truly want to be, no matter where we are today. Whether we like it or not, just as the world around us is evolving and changing into something new every single day, so are we, as individuals. Assess yourself. Assess your behaviors. Assess your results. If you can be easy on yourself when you don't like the choice you've made, gently nudge yourself back to the direction you wish for next time. Do this for every area of your life, and you are a success *today*. There is no destination. If you can live today with this presence, what you have or don't have in life—including confidence—won't seem quite as important. Don't stand in your own way. You'll end up with more than you ever dreamed of, as long as you trust the process. Your deepest insecurity is precisely the path to your biggest success. Will you activate the courage to face it?

ACKNOWLEDGMENTS

This book was thirty-six years in the making. There are so many people in my life who have contributed tremendously to the lessons I learned, many of which were shared in this book. I owe a debt of gratitude to so many of you.

My wife, Avarey. You have always encouraged me to be myself and to listen to my gut. I bet you had no idea the ride I would take you on when you married me. Who I am today would barely be recognized by the person I was when you married me, and yet with patience, you still accept, love, and encourage me to move in the direction of my dreams.

Richard Robbins, my coach, my mentor, my second dad, and my friend. You are the reason I had a book to write. Not only did you introduce me to most of the philosophies that I share, but you taught me to be a better husband, dad, friend, and businessperson. You taught me to think bigger, and most of all, you inadvertently helped me build my self-assurance.

David Irvine. When a strange young kid whom you'd never met walked up to you in a conference to ask you for help in writing a book, you showed no hesitation and even invited me into your home, then eventually into your life. Your eloquence in teaching others about authenticity is second to none. You live your calling, and it inspires me to do the same. We need more people like you.

Ron Lefebvre. You're the only person I know who challenges himself and his friends more than I do. You inspire me to keep pushing myself, and I'm blessed to know you.

Pierre Blais. My Death Race running partner. The one who wouldn't let me run the last leg of GCDR for a bonus round because you knew I probably would have collapsed! I was so mad at you for holding me back! Though you understand and share my intensity, you keep me from going too far sometimes. Thanks for balancing me. Thanks for all the conversations about my book before it was one. You helped it come to life.

Marc, Maurice, and Claudette Carriere. You let a rebellious young kid come into your home and made him feel like a part of the family when I didn't feel like I had one. When

I didn't feel like I belonged anywhere else, I always felt safe in the Carriere house. Thank you.

Paul Blais. I was a lone wolf until you showed me that accomplishing big things is much easier to do when you partner with good people and form a common goal. Your generosity and constant encouragement to get me out to conferences led me to meeting the people who became crucial in helping me finish this book.

Ron Dickson. My business partner and my friend. When I have no confidence, you lend me yours. Our story didn't make it into this book, but perhaps it's because we aren't done writing that story yet.

2J Pantoja. You continue to teach me to release my inhibitions and to trust myself every day. You make no apologies for who you are, and you teach me to do the same for myself.

Tucker Max, Hal Clifford, and Emily Gindlesparger (and the entire team at Scribe Media). Your genius in helping people like me in self-publishing is mind-blowing. You make the complex simple. You make the abstract real, and you created a community of authors that helps make everything just a little easier.

My mother, Diane Christensen. Though we never agreed

on much, you being who you are taught me strength and resilience. You taught me to have tough conversations when they were needed, and you taught me the value of making a true decision. You showed me to never give up on anything I start.

My father, Jean Amyotte. You lived a crazier life than anyone I know, and sharing your story in my book wouldn't have done it justice. Perhaps one day you'll write a book of your own. You weren't around to watch me become the man I am today, but as Ron Dickson often reminded me, you carried the cross so I could become the person I've become. I made it my mission not to let the lessons of your challenges go to waste.